Belly Dancing

FOR FITNESS

Belly Dancing

FOR FITNESS

THE SEXY ART THAT TONES YOUR ABS, BUM AND THIGHS

BY RANIA ANDRONIKI BOSSONIS

Text © 2004 by Rania Bossonis

Published in the UK in 2004 by
Apple Press
Sheridan House
112-116A Western Road
Hove
East Sussex BN3 1DD
England
www.apple-press.com

10 9 8 7 6 5 4 3 2 1

ISBN 1-84092-475-6

Cover design by Ariana Dingman
Book production by Laura McFadden

Printed and bound in Singapore

This book is dedicated to my father, Andreas Evangelos Bossonis, for believing in me and encouraging me to be an artist.

Contents

Introduction

My Dance Biography

I will never, ever forget the first time I witnessed a belly-dance performance. I remember every small detail: her costume, her hair, her makeup, the way the parts of her body moved independently of each other, like instruments that make up an orchestra, perfectly conveying the music. She was like a walking drum kit. I had never seen anything so cool in my life, and since I was only eight years old, it left quite an impression on me. It was at a Greek restaurant in Yonkers, New York, on an Easter Sunday, and it also marked the first and only time we (my family) ever had Greek Easter dinner at a place other than at our family table. I wanted to grow up and be just like her. So I did.

It was six years later that I saw my next dancer. I was a freshman in high school and had taken a part-time job that was about forty minutes from my house by bus, in a part of town I was not all that familiar with. While waiting for a bus home, I noticed posters adorning the window of a restaurant, advertising the arrival of a famous bellydancer. I don't know what came over me, but I walked inside and told the manager that I wanted to become a bellydancer, and asked if I could buy a ticket. He must have been moved by my enthusiasm, as he offered to let me see the show for free if I sat at the bar (so as not to take up the valuable real estate of a table), and ordered a few sodas. We shook hands as if we had made some business deal.

I don't remember her name, but I remember everything else. Her costume; her elegant, sophisticated demeanor; her dress; and how she was just as good as the first dancer that I had seen, but her style was totally different. I learned then that the first dancer I had seen was dancing the very fast Greek/Turkish style, while this dancer was trained in the Egyptian style, which is quite different, like the difference between jazz and modern dance.

The restaurant was filled to capacity that night, with many people standing after all the seats had been taken. Large families came and sat at tables of twelve and sixteen people. I felt very lucky to be there. People were giving twenty-dollar bills to the waiters, which the waiters would change into stacks of single dollars that the people would throw up into the air above the dancer so that it was "raining" money on her. Every few minutes, someone would come with a broom and sweep up the money. I thought to myself, "Wow, she must be really rich."

The two gentlemen sitting next to me at the bar told me that many of the Middle Eastern people in the neighborhood would come to see this dancer whenever she came to their town, because she danced just like some of the famous dancers from "back home." They told me that in Egypt and Lebanon, bellydancing is part of their culture that grew out of traditional dance, and that the dancers appear on television and in movies, dancing to thirty-five-piece orchestras in large theaters.

One of the things that made this particular dancer different from the first one I had seen was that she incorporated balancing in her act. About halfway through the show, she left the stage for about one minute while the band played. She returned with a different costume, and she was balancing a large silver tray filled with burning votive candles. The music had slowed down considerably, as did her dancing. While balancing the tray, she was able to do a full split, as well as many other difficult steps, while still maintaining graceful, flowing movement to the music.

I went to her dressing room afterward, where she was standing over her mountain of dollar bills with the manager, trying to arrange them into piles and count them. I told her that I was going to learn how to bellydance. She stopped what she was doing, looked me up and down, nodded her approval, and said, "Okay. Well, I wish you success for your future. It takes a lot of training, you know."

The very next day I consulted my trusty New York Yellow Pages and found Serena's School of Middle Eastern Dance in Manhattan. I purchased a dance card and took two classes on the first day. I loved it. It would be safe to say that I was addicted. Serena was telling the class about her most recent trip to Egypt, and about a performance she did in which she was dressed as Nefertiti (the ancient Egyptian goddess). I loved learning about the cultural origins of the movements just as much as I loved learning the movements themselves. Bellydancing came easily for me, as I could find many similarities between its moves and some of the moves from Greek social dances that I had learned growing up. I studied for about two years, then went away to college.

I never forgot what I had learned. I practiced at home several times a week, perhaps as some sort of therapy. After college, I pursued a career in photography and computer graphics, all the while still bellydancing regularly in my living room.

It did not take a scientist to figure out that this was great exercise. My job in computer graphics involved sitting glued to a computer for eight- to ten-hour days, with no exercise. For a few years, my only exercise was dancing in my living room for twenty minutes, three to four times per week. I was in dynamite shape. I had muscle tone, definition, flexibility, and stamina. And I had fun.

By then I had relocated from New York to Connecticut, where it seemed that suddenly there was not one bellydancer to be found. I looked in telephone directories and asked around, but I could not find one person with similar interests. I just kept practicing at home, but I really wanted to continue studying the dance. I took occasional road trips to New York and Boston to spend a day taking classes with Serena, Yousri Sharif, Katia, or Phaedra.

One day a new person was hired at my job, and we were talking about hobbies. When I mentioned bellydancing, her face lit up as she told me she knew a lady who was not only a professional dancer, but who also owned a bellydance agency. She scribbled a phone number and the name Nancy on a piece of paper and said, "You should call her."

I called Nancy and told her I was interested in taking lessons. She told me I had to audition, which really intimidated me. I practiced for two days straight, then went to the audition. Nancy (stage name, "Natasha") was very nice to me, but there was still something intimidating about auditioning in front of a professional.

She played some music by George Abdo and told me to dance right there in her living room. I was quite nervous at first, but eventually I loosened up as I got involved in the nuances of the music. It seemed like a very long time, but the duration was only one song.

When I finished, Nancy smiled and asked me who my teacher was. When I said, "Serena," Nancy said, "I can see some of Serena in you." Then she shocked the living daylights out of me by telling me that she was hiring me as a professional dancer, and that she had a show for me in two days.

Sheherezat

I panicked, thinking I couldn't possibly be ready. "I don't have a costume," I said, hoping that would get me out of it. She wrote down two phone numbers and handed them to me. One number was for her daughter Lisa, who happened to be the same size as me and had some used costumes to sell. The other number was for her friend Nicole Michaud, who was teaching bellydance. I studied with Nicole for at least a year, every Saturday morning. She taught me a lot about technique, costuming, and stage dynamics, and she introduced me to the Egyptian style.

I bought two costumes from Lisa (stage name, "Sheherezat"), who was an amazing dancer. She danced Turkish style, with speed, agility, and power. She was a brilliant performer and a brilliant person in general. She worked her way through eight years of veterinary college by bellydancing on the weekends. It was her only form of exercise as well, and she had a beautiful figure, with a perfectly flat stomach.

The rest is history. Sheherezat, Natasha, and I became great friends over the years. Natasha had me doing between three and six shows per week. Still to this day, I have never stopped studying the dance feverishly, taking lessons whenever a famous teacher is in the area, buying videos, and so on. With 5,000 years of history behind it, one could begin studying Middle Eastern dance and never finish learning all there is to learn in one lifetime.

All the performing and studying paid off when I moved to California. I was trying to meet other dancers and get involved in the local dance community, so I signed up to compete in the Bellydancer of the Universe Competition: the first, largest, and, in my opinion, the most difficult competition of its kind. Honestly, I did not think that I would win, I thought I would meet people and make friends and get some good constructive criticism from the judges. I was in shock when they announced me as the winner. When I walked to the stage to receive the award, I felt like I was floating. I couldn't sleep that night; I kept staring across the room at the two enormous trophies I had won, trying to make sure it had really happened. Winning really helped my confidence, which, prior to that point, was about halfway between low and normal. I entered the competition again in 2002 and also took the championship.

It seemed like some strange dream, but suddenly the phone never stopped ringing with requests for performances. Every time I did a show, several people would call and say, "I saw you at the show last week for Omar's birthday, and want to know if you're available to perform at my daughter's wedding" and so on. Soon, I was steadily working an average of ten shows per week, and teaching four to five bellydance classes per week. Somehow, I was not tired of it.

By then I was in the best shape I had ever been in. People constantly stopped me and asked what type of workout I did. When I replied that I just bellydance often, they would always ask, "But don't you lift weights or do sit-ups, also?" And my response would be no because if I were to lift weights, I would be too sore to dance the next day. I was dancing so frequently that I couldn't afford to have sore abs from doing sit-ups, or sore shoulders or legs from lifting weights.

At this point it was unavoidably clear just how beneficial bellydance is as a form of exercise. I also noticed the vast age range of students attending my classes. It was not uncommon for a sixty-five-year-old grandmother to attend a class alongside her eight-year-old granddaughter. There were many mother and daughter attendees, as well as junior high school and high school students, and a large number of students in the age range of twenty-five to forty. Bellydancing is not only great exercise, it can be utilized at any age and still produce benefits to the body, such as improved posture, coordination, strength, and flexibility.

I got the idea to produce a workout video using bellydance movements I felt produced great physical results, such as Camels and Snake Arms. I became an

AFAA-certified fitness instructor, then emptied my savings account and made my first bellydance workout video, the *Exotic Bellydance Workout*. A company that produces workout videos saw the tape and hired me to create and star in a series of videos/DVDs titled *Bellydance Fitness for Weight Loss*. Since then, I have shifted my focus slightly to teaching more, performing less (only three to four shows per week), and self-producing some advanced bellydance technique and choreography videos.

I must add that although I love dancing, there are times when it can be difficult emotionally, especially when dealing with public misconceptions about the dance. There are many people who are unfamiliar with Middle Eastern dance, and they equate it with stripping. This dance really has nothing to do with stripping. When the dance is done properly, the audience should be mesmerized by the skill of the dancer and immersed in her choreography and interpretation of the music. It takes years to become polished enough as a dancer to be able to achieve this goal. There are, unfortunately, many people who study bellydancing and think they are ready to perform after a few short months. The result is a dance that looks jerky and sometimes vulgar, since their skills are not refined and smooth yet. I think one half of the misconceptions about this dance come from people having never seen a bellydancer perform and imagining it to be like stripping, and the other fifty percent come from people who saw an amateur performing as if she were a professional.

I am glad to be living in an era in which VCRs are common to most households, and professional bellydance videotapes are available to the mass market, so more people can have access to quality bellydance performances.

This book will touch on many aspects of Middle Eastern dance, or bellydancing, including its history, music, and costuming, and the different styles and movements, exercises, steps, and combinations. I hope you enjoy this book, and most of all, I hope you appreciate this art form for its historical, physical, and stress-relieving qualities.

Chapter 1 | *The Many Benefits of Bellydancing*

Bellydancing offers a different approach to movement than what is traditionally taught by Western cultures. After studying bellydancing, the accomplished student will have improved coordination, balance, muscle tone, and posture. Aside from the physical benefits, there are social and mental/emotional benefits such as stress reduction, meeting people with a similar interest, a feeling of satisfaction from mastering a new skill, and learning the history of how this remarkable art form evolved.

Low-Impact and High-Impact Aerobics

The feminine, glitzy, cabaret style of bellydance, which most people are familiar with, is predominantly low-impact aerobic exercise, if performed without stopping for the standard minimum of the twenty minutes it takes for the body to achieve an aerobic benefit. Hence the many titles of bellydance workout videos on the market today. (I, too, am guilty, with eight bellydance fitness videos of my own.) It really is great exercise.

When you add some of the more folkloric steps such as Debke, Saidi, or Turkish Karsilama, the dance becomes high-impact aerobics. For those not familiar, low-impact workouts cause very little stress to the feet, shins, knees, and so forth, and can be performed by almost anyone. High-impact aerobics involve more jumping and, although they are the ultimate method of calorie burning, should be avoided by people who are prone to shin splints, knee problems, or plantar fasciitis.

Shimmy Away the Fat

Many people are paying high prices to go to spas and receive vacumobilization treatments, which "mobilize" fat cells and cellulite areas that normally don't receive much action. This process is also said to help detoxify and promote lymphatic drainage. Sounds wonderful, but why would you pay someone to shake your fat around, when you can just shimmy for five minutes per day?

Shimmying naturally invigorates and improves circulation to all areas of the body, particularly the thighs, buttocks, and abdomen. Depending on your arm position, it will also hit that flabby area at the underside of the upper arm.

Benefits of Isolation Exercises

The isolation exercises teach us to be able to use and control all of our individual muscles, not just tighten them. Repeating the isolation exercises for each area of the body results in visually beautiful muscle definition, though different from the chiseled, hard look of a bodybuilder.

Learning the isolation movements of the head, neck, and shoulders will benefit anyone who stores tension in this area. When we become tense, the neck and shoulders become stiff, as though all the muscles were stuck together into one body part. People that store tension in the neck and shoulders often cannot move their shoulders without moving their neck, and vice versa, as they have lost flexibility and control in that region. After several weeks of working on Snake Arms, Shoulder Shimmies,

Head Slides, and Khaleegy Head Rolls, you will notice more flexibility, less tension, and more control. After practicing, it will be easy for you to command your shoulders to move without moving your neck.

What would happen to your neck if you did not exercise it at all? Would it sag and age prematurely? Probably. One thing I love about bellydance is that it gently works all areas of the body. I could take step aerobics classes consistently for years, but although my body would be in great shape, I would not have worked the muscles in my neck once.

Bellydancing Tones Your Abs

Although almost all muscle groups—such as the arms, neck, ribs, hips, pelvis, buttocks, hands, and even facial expressions—are isolated and controlled in Middle Eastern dance, let's take a moment to focus on the abdominal region.

Let's face it, a vast majority of people consider a "six-pack" torso a very desirable trait. Most typically the exercises (and exercise equipment) used to achieve a well-defined abdomen serve only to tighten the abdominal muscle group. Few people actually develop their abdominals in such a way that they can control muscle movement in the region.

I can command my fingers to grasp an object; I can command my legs to perform ballet exercises. Why would I want my abdominal muscles to be able to do nothing but remain as tight as possible? Can this be healthy?

Let's take a quick look at some other philosophies concerning the subject. Tai Chi teaches ab exercises that extend, stretch, and even "roll" the abdominals to effectively distribute Chi energy throughout the body, as well as to massage the internal organs, which is said to stimulate digestion and boost metabolism. Various forms of yoga teach similar techniques of rolling the abdominals for the same reasons. Yoga takes exercises in the abdominal region very seriously. In fact, not only can one learn the basic downward- or upward-rolling yoga technique, but one can also learn sideways rolling and a Belly Circle, where instead of rolling, the abdominal muscles move in a complete circle, like a Ferris wheel. Several childbirth-preparation techniques teach the basic Belly Roll and abdominal isolation techniques to prepare a woman's abdomen for contractions during labor so she can move with the contractions rather than be tense and resist them.

In his book *Optimal Wellness*, Ralph Golan, M.D., recommends raising the arms above the head to lift abdominal muscles, as well as "making rhythmic downward rolls of your abdominal muscles" to advance stool downward without straining for individuals suffering from constipation. Straining can create dangerous internal pressure, and the Belly Roll helps to prevent straining and assists in helping the patient relax and focus.

Bellydance is perhaps the only dance form that teaches these abdominal exercises, primarily because bellydancing is over 5,000 years old and has evolved to reflect many ancient customs and rituals from the Middle Eastern region, including movements from childbirth-preparation exercises and fertility rituals. It was (and, in some areas, still is) common for young girls to learn belly-rolling techniques, which involve both stretching and outward pushing, and the tightening of the rectus abdominus and diaphram, as preparation for childbirth. Let's think about the basic logic here: during pregnancy, a woman's abdominal muscles and skin will stretch to many times greater than normal size in a matter of a few short months. If her stomach muscles and skin have never before been stretched at all, this will be quite traumatic to the body, and will be difficult to recover from. However, if she has trained her abdomen for years to extend/stretch outward and then tighten from a stretched position, it will be much easier for her muscles and skin to stretch during pregnancy, as well as to recover from the extreme stretch after childbirth. How this brilliant exercise concept became merged with dance is unclear, but I am grateful nonetheless.

Furthermore, it is important to consider that crunches and sit-ups will not work your waistline. In order to sculpt and tone the waistline, you must engage the muscles at the sides of the waist, such as the obliques and intercostals. Bellydance exercises that work the hips, waist, and rib cage effectively stretch, build, and tone the waistline.

Benefits of Undulations

The snakelike undulations stretch and strengthen opposing muscle groups simultaneously. Performing Arm Undulations (commonly called Snake Arms) tones all the muscles in the arms, including the hard-to-reach area at the underside of the upper arm. Also, this exercise will increase flexibility of the shoulders and help reduce stiffness in the upper back, which is especially important for those individuals who store tension in their neck and upper back. Doing full-body undulations, or Camels, both stretches and strengthens the Rectus Abdominus and Erector Spinae (the entire column of both abdominal and spinal muscles). Whether you choose to pursue bellydancing or not, practicing full-body undulations will give you a stronger, flatter stomach and better posture, will reduce or eliminate lower back problems, and will strengthen and increase flexibility of the spine. I highly recommend this exercise, especially for those of us who spend long hours driving or sitting at a desk or computer, where the lower vertebrae can become compressed and cause chronic pain. Also, hand undulations and hand circles (all of these exercises are described in later chapters in detail) are recommended for typists and musicians who may be prone to repetitive motion disorder, as these exercises work all the muscles in the wrist in the full range of motion.

Healthy Basic Posture

We have discussed how you can easily see an improvement in your posture from all the wonderful undulations and isolations. But let's focus now on another aspect of posture: the basic posture of bellydancing. The basic posture one assumes to perform the dance correctly involves having the feet directly under the hips (not wide apart at all), even support in the legs without locking the knees, a Pelvic Tuck (pelvis tucked slightly beneath the torso, as opposed to being hyperextended and protruding), a slight lift in the chest and support from the abdominals, and head looking straight forward. This posture is very natural and essentially healthy to all areas of the body.

When I was a child, I spent several years studying gymnastics, where one finishes each routine by assuming a gymnastic pose, in which the head looks up. I learned much later in life that this posture places undue stress on the vertebrae of the neck. I took hip-hop dance classes and found that this dance form involves a lot of hyperextension of the lower back. One who studies ballet will notice the turned-out position of the legs is predominant. These dance forms are great for young, supple bodies. As one gets older, she or he may eventually have to leave these dance forms behind. An older person probably could not consider beginning to study one of these dance forms.

By contrast, we find the basic posture of Middle Eastern dance to be very easy and natural to the body, so, theoretically, as long as one can walk, one can keep bellydancing. I have had many, many students who took their first bellydance class in their forties and fifties and continue bellydancing for years. I know one dancer who began studying bellydance at age fifty, after she had hip surgery. She hoped to strengthen muscles around her hips through bellydance. She immediately fell in love with the dance, and within a few years became accomplished enough to be a professional. She had speed, agility, and wonderful stage presence. By the time she was sixty, she was touring retirement homes across the United States, performing and teaching bellydancing for seniors.

Variety of Subject Matter

There really is no such thing as just learning bellydance, since the term "bellydance" is a nickname that encompasses a variety of dances such as Egyptian, Lebanese and Debke, Persian, Saidi, Saudi Arabian, Turkish, Zar, Tunisian, Shamadan, Cane dance, and others, to name a few. So, to actually study the dance, one could spend an entire lifetime learning techniques and traditions from various parts of the world. Believe me, this makes time fly during class. Sure, you are dancing and exercising, but the rich and diverse history of this unique subject is an added educational benefit.

Learning New Music and Cultures

To study bellydancing in depth would inevitably lead to learning a wide variety of rhythms, time signatures, and instruments that define music from the different cultures and countries that comprise bellydance. (I know, I know. The music all sounds the same at first, but it truly is quite varied. Hopefully, the enclosed music CD will provide a good introduction to the music used for bellydance.) Hand in hand with learning music comes learning the traditional steps that are performed to each type of music.

Stress Reduction

There is definitely a "Zen" element to bellydancing, as it requires both physical effort and mental focus. After all, it is your mind that must command all those muscle groups to move in isolation and opposition to one another, all the while keeping track of the music and choreography. The combination of exercise and concentration results in a great tool for stress reduction. Also, there is a strong element of self-expression in bellydancing, which enables the dancer to let her emotions come through in her dancing. What better way to let it all out?

Self-Expression

Although the basic movements are taught much the same way to everyone, it seems that no two bellydancers dance alike. Perhaps it is because of the internal nature of the movements themselves, but it is an interesting phenomenon nonetheless. You may frequently hear reference to a dancer's "style." It is encouraged in bellydance for each person to learn the moves correctly but find her own way of presenting them in choreography or combinations that reflect her own self-expression. I observed a bellydance competition where all the contestants were given the same piece of music to dance to. It was simply astounding to see how each dancer interpreted the music completely differently! There were not two dancers who were even close to each other. Once you have mastered the basics, choose which movements and steps are your favorites, and try building your own choreography.

Female Bonding

My classes are composed of 99 percent women. Why is this? Mainly because the bellydancing that is performed in costume is really a stylized, feminine version of folkloric steps. One could argue that it was tailored specifically for women. When men dance the traditional steps, they wear regular clothes or traditional clothes; it is a completely different dance. It is not typical at all, actually it is rare, for a man to perform a bellydance routine the same way as a woman does. I can name only a handful of male bellydancers, though I hear that there is a more abundant supply of them in Turkey during recent years. There exists a much larger number of men who study folkloric dances such as Saidi (Upper Egypt) and Debke (Lebanese, Arabic, or Turkish traditional), who may pursue those specific genres and perform with a group. I must note here that some of the best bellydance teachers and choreographers are men (Yousri Sharif Yousri, Ibrahim Farrah, Ibrahim Akef, Momo Kaduos, Amir Thaleb, Horatio Cifuentes, etc.). They understand the feminine bellydance and are highly skilled at it, but it is simply not common or popular for a man to perform the feminine version of the dance. I once took a choreography seminar with Amir Thaleb, and he taught us flawlessly the feminine version of his choreography. Then, he performed the same choreography in the masculine style. The difference between the two styles was obvious, and only a master such as Amir Thaleb could have done both perfectly.

If you have ever seen a Hawaiian dance performance, you may recognize the same dynamic. The female hula dancers wear a feminine costume and perform their steps,

Sharif, an Egyptian dance teacher and choreographer.

and although they dance with men, the men are wearing a masculine costume and performing a more masculine version of the dance, sometimes using sticks and fire as props.

Thus, the bellydance classroom finds itself largely populated by women and is widely accepted among women as a great place to bond with other women and explore the very feminine exercises and glamorous costuming of bellydancing, and just be in a feminine space. New friends are frequently made, and many a Girls' Night Out is planned after class.

Exploring Femininity/Sensuality

Learning to bellydance involves learning to move muscles in your body that you have never used before; to become very aware of and in tune with your body. I sometimes wonder if this is the main reason that women are compelled to try it, as well as being the reason it is viewed as sensual. For many women who have grown up in American society, especially those without a dance background, the belly-dance class may be the first time in their lives they are encouraged to think about their own body awareness, and to pay attention to all the parts of their bodies (let alone for the intention of creating a beautiful dance). It is a forum where women are encouraged to learn control of their bodies in a beautiful, graceful way. Perhaps the self-awareness, graceful control, and small, internal movements are the essence of bellydance's sensual appeal: that the bellydancer took the time to develop every part of her body and to present the movement in a dance shows her intense mind-body connection.

Personal Achievement

There are not words sufficient in the English language to describe the feeling of being able to move one's body in a way previously only dreamed about. Bellydance exercises feel awkward at first. Really awkward. I tell my beginning students, "If it feels weird, it probably looks good." This makes sense if you consider that this is a different type of movement than we are accustomed to. So, if it feels familiar, it probably is not correct. Nonetheless, as a beginning student, it is hard to imagine being able to accomplish any level of success. I remember when I could do three barrel turns in a row, and I felt proud that I could do three. Now I can do thirty-three without skipping a beat. I remember when I could shimmy for only about five seconds straight, and it seemed like an eternity. Now, I could go for ten minutes and not feel it. As any bodybuilder will tell you, the body welcomes new physical challenges and responds by getting stronger. A little practice can go a long way!

One could study bellydancing for one's entire life and still achieve new levels of mastery. And I hope you do!

This is the artist's rendering
of Maude Allen's famous
Salome costume.

Chapter 2 | *A Brief History of Bellydance*

Angelika Nemeth

What Is Bellydance?

Bellydance is a form of dance that originated in the Middle East. It is characterized by articulated isolation movements, undulations, intricate patterns of hip isolations, ribbonlike arm and torso undulations, percussive locking movements, circular hand movements, and shaking or fluttering movements (shimmies). Facial expressions are used to convey the meaning of the song, be they soulful or joyful, as dancers are expected to "feel" the music and express emotion to the audience. Exceptional control and use of the stomach should also be noted, as almost all movements, even walking movements, originate from the stomach.

This dance was once nicknamed "danse du ventre" (dance of the stomach) by the French; hence, the poorly translated term "bellydance." Another common name for the dance is Beledi, meaning, "dance from the country," which refers to the folkloric dance style of the countryside of Upper Egypt, from which many modern bellydance movements stem. Another name for the dance is Raks Sharqi (pronounced Raks Shar-key), which means "dance of the East."

Origins and Evolution of the Dance

Rich and diverse in its background, bellydance is thousands of years old. It originated in the Middle East and North Africa and is one of the oldest dance forms. It is amazing to sit back and imagine that when people first began to dance, these are some of the movements that they intuitively chose to use. When people first began drumming, clapping, and chanting, this is how they chose to interpret the music and express themselves. Aside from being intuitive, it is natural for the body.

Some elements of the dance predate monotheism, stemming from early rituals for celebration, healing, trance, and exorcism. It may seem hard to imagine, but before monotheism, early matriarchal cultures believed women's bodies were sacred for their ability to give birth. There were birthing rituals and exercises to prepare young women for the physical stress of childbirth. Aside from temple dances, there were also folk dances that were social in nature.

Eventually, Judaism, Christianity, and Islam rose and did away with temple dances and fertility rituals. Almost overnight, dance and the female body were no longer sacred.

Well, the folk dances remained, and they incorporated movements that harkened back to the old temple dances. As the folk dances spread throughout different regions, they took on different characteristics and flavors, and developed more fully to reflect their surrounding cultures. Gypsies that traveled the "Gypsy Trail" from India to Spain and Europe influenced many regions along the way with their music and dance. Each region of the Middle East and North Africa developed its own style of folkloric dance, music, and costume, although many common elements exist among them. There are Saidi and Beledi (Egypt); Khaleegy (Saidi Arabian Gulf); Debke (Lebanon); Karsilama (Turkey); Chiftitelli (Greek); Tunisian, Persian, and Nubian dance, and many more. Elements of these folkloric dances would evolve into what we know today as bellydance.

Bellydance Hits the United States

In 1893, Sol Bloom created an exhibition of Middle Eastern dance and culture at the Chicago World's Fair, which depicted a scene from an Algerian village. It was here that the nickname "bellydance" was first coined (probably as an interpretation of the French *danse du ventre*). Authentic dancers imported from the Middle East performed their hip shimmies, undulations, and gyrations for a shocked, outraged, and entirely curious crowd of straightlaced Victorian-era Americans. Soon, bellydance was in the newspapers and on the lips of people across America, due either to outrage or fascination with the Middle Eastern dance. Little Egypt, a dancer who performed at this exhibition, became a household name as Little Egypt imitators soon sprang up everywhere.

Around the same time, "Salomania" hit the United States. After Oscar Wilde's play *Salomé* was published, fascination with this biblical dancer swept the nation. Maude Allen performed a famous dance depicting Salome, wearing an exotic costume of bra and belt covered with jewels and pearls, over a sheer, flowing skirt.

Maude Allen's costume would later typify what other Salome and Little Egypt imitators would wear, and thus create an expectation of what a "bellydancer" should look like. Costumes of dancers in the Middle East would then change to meet the expectations of Western tourists, who would spend money on trips to the Middle East. (I guess we couldn't disappoint them by letting them find out that Middle Eastern women did not really dress like Maude Allen.)

Ritual Dances

Some ritual dances still exist today. Sufism is considered by many to be an esoteric branch of Islam (although many Muslims contend that the Sufis are considered outside the scope of Islam). Sufis perform religious whirling dervish (continuous rhythmic spinning) dances to connect with God through motion, trance, and rhythm. Also, the ancient Zar exorcism dance, which involves repetitive circling motions of the head (until evil spirits are cast out), is still performed to this day. Zar rhythm (Ayoub) and movements are sometimes included in Middle Eastern dance compositions.

ABOVE: Whirling Dervish performed in Aswan Egypt. LEFT: Sufi dancers in Cairo, Egypt.

The Golden Era of Entertainment in Egypt

In 1927, Badia Masabni founded Casino Opera in Egypt, an upscale nightclub with an orchestra and dancing show. She worked with such dancers as Tahia Karioka and Samia Gamal to refine the folkloric steps by adding poised arm and foot positions and choreography to elevate the dance from its earthy folkloric roots and adapt it to the stage.

During the 1940s, Egypt experienced a golden age of cinematography, inspired by Hollywood. Some of Egypt's greatest films and music would be produced during this time, with elaborate sets, gorgeous costumes, and choreographed musical and dance numbers. The dancers from the Casino Opera became stars throughout the entire Middle East, as they sang, danced, and acted in these great classic films. By this time, the Egyptian style of dance had fully evolved to be different from the Turkish and Arabic styles.

In 1959, Mahmoud Reda, an Olympic gold medalist in gymnastics from Egypt, founded the Reda Dance Troupe in Cairo. Reda's use of elegant costuming with beautiful, dynamic group choreography gained recognition in films and theaters throughout the Middle East. Many of Egypt's most famous dance soloists such as Farida Fahmy and Dina began their careers in Reda's troupe.

Carioka Caridea

Meanwhile, Back in the U.S.A.

Back in the United States, the dance was changing and evolving as well. By the mid-1960s, night clubs that catered to a melting pot of ethnic immigrants such as Greeks, Turks, Armenians, Egyptians, Lebanese, Syrians, and others were sprouting up in major cities. These nightclubs created a demand in America for bellydancers who could appeal to multiethnic audiences. Women who studied it as a hobby suddenly found themselves working as career bellydancers.

As bellydance continued to appeal to American women, dancers traveled to the Middle East to become better educated. A scholarly and highly intelligent dancer named Morocco (a.k.a. Carolina Varga Dinicu) made frequent educational trips to the Middle East. During one such trip, she smuggled herself into a private function to witness firsthand an actual Berber birthing ritual. Her widely published writings of this and other accounts further helped Westerners to understand the origins of Middle Eastern dance and break away from the scandalous "hootchy-kootchy" stereotypes of the late 1800s.

Bellydance teachers opened schools, and more and more dancers were trained. Dancers began to choose which styles appealed to them most: American cabaret, Turkish, Arabic/Lebanese, or Egyptian. Instructors like Ibrahim "Bobby" Farrah traveled from the Middle East to teach scores of dancers all over the world. Not only did schools develop, but organizations such as the Middle Eastern Culture and Dance Association (MECDA) were formed to provide dancers with a code of ethics and sources of information.

Bellydance made it to the collegiate level when Angelika Nemeth began teaching Middle Eastern dance at Orange Coast College in Southern California in 1977. This program has expanded to become the OCC World Dance Certificate program, a program so successful that its student recitals are actually sold-out concerts with critically acclaimed reviews. Along with her colleagues Sahra Kent and Shareen el Safy, Angelika made Orange Coast College part of Middle Eastern dance history by producing and hosting the Annual International Conference on Middle Eastern Dance, featuring lectures, classes, and performances from legendary dance figures.

Bellydance became popular in other countries as well, in places such as Germany, England, Australia, and South America. Beata and Horatio Cifuentes, two former ballet dancers, have Middle Eastern dance instruction schools in Germany and produce large theater shows, videos, and festivals. In Brazil, a dancer named Hyat Al Helwa opened a chain of successful schools for Middle Eastern dance. She currently has eight schools, and she also organizes large dance festivals, which bring Middle Eastern dancers from all over the world to Brazil.

Recently, bellydance popularity has exploded worldwide, perhaps largely due to accessibility through media such as videotapes, DVDs, and the Internet. Fitness instructors began to realize the many health benefits of bellydance, which led to the vast array of bellydance fitness-program videos. Who would have thought one could find bellydance in Kmart? Times most certainly have changed. After the success of bellydance workout videos, distributors began releasing performance videos and DVDs to the mainstream market, to much success. As I am typing these words, Miles Copeland of Ark 21 Records is managing the first-ever Bellydance Superstars U.S. tour.

Ozel Turkbas album covers from the 1960s.

A Look at Some of the Different Styles of Bellydance

MODERN EGYPTIAN

Contemporary version of Egyptian dance that grew out of the traditional Beledi dance. Refined, feminine, small internal movements; emotional facial expressions; and some elements of ballet (lots of demi-pointe) make this dance very popular. Walking and posing steps, intricate hip movements, and a coquettish air also characterize this style. Much of the movement focuses on isolations in the trunk of the body. Dancers such as Lucy, Mona Al Said, Nagwa Fouad, and Sohair Zaky were the reigning queens of Egyptian dance throughout the 1970s and 1980s, while Dina is perhaps today's most popular dancer in Cairo. Teacher Raqia Hassan travels all over the world teaching her modern Egyptian technique and choreography.

Nagwa Fouad, Egyptian Dancer

ABOVE: Eva Cernick,
Turkish-style dancer

TURKISH

Closer to the Gypsy roots of bellydance, the Turkish style is faster, livelier, and earthier than its Egyptian cousin. Movements are larger and more athletic. Dancers express joy and celebration and perform moves that show off their flexibility and stamina. Movements and energy are less focused in the trunk, often extending throughout the entire body. An occasional jump or series of movements on the floor adds a wide dynamic range to this dance vocabulary. It is also common to add some folkloric Karsilama steps to a 9/8 rhythm at the end of a cabaret dance routine.

Ozel Turkbas, a dancer from Turkey, is often credited with bringing the Turkish style to America in the early 1960s. She produced several albums of bellydance music, complete with printed dance instruction manuals. There are many dancers linked to this genre, two of the most popular being Elizabeth Artemis Mourat and Eva Cernick. Eva was one of my very first influences, because she could be at the same time strong, fast, right on time with the music, yet delicate and feminine. Artemis Mourat is known not only for her authentic Turkish dancing, but also for her extensive research and writings on the topic.

MODERN LEBANESE

It is often speculated that the Lebanese style of bellydance blends elements from both the Turkish and Egyptian styles. Contemporary Lebanese bellydancers wear glitzy cabaret costumes with high-heeled dance shoes. Some dancers contend that part of the unique flavor of modern Lebanese dance comes from the effect the high heels have on the basic body position/posture; because the heels push the weight of the body forward, the mechanics of even the most basic of moves have been altered. Lebanon's most famous dancers are Nadia Gamal, Amany, and Samara. Bellydancing is so popular in Lebanon that bellydancers are a routine part of television programming there.

AMERICAN CABARET

This style originated in the multiethnic clubs that sprang up during the 1960s in America, such as Haji Baba in New York and the Fez in Los Angeles. Different Middle Eastern and Western dance styles were blended to appeal to an audience of immigrants from many different countries from the Middle East and Mediterranean, such as Turkey, Greece, Armenia, Lebanon, Syria, and so on. Not only were styles blended together, but also the lack of formal bellydance education in America at the time led to much improvising, making the dance look similar but different from the actual Middle Eastern dance. American dancers placed more emphasis on the use of the veil as a prop.

AMERICAN TRIBAL

The idea for this fascinating art form was born when Jamila Salimpour's Bal Anat troupe abandoned the glitzy, sequined cabaret costumes in search of the dance's ethnic roots. In the mid-1980s, Carolena Nericcio created the FatChanceBelly Dance troupe, which sparked the fast-growing Tribal dance style. I hate to use clichés, but Tribal dance really did catch on like wildfire. It was as though dancers were thirsty for something completely different. Tribal dance costumes draw on elements from Pakistani, Indian, Afghan, North African, and Arabic costume and jewelry. They wear turbans, Afghan jewelry, bindis, and henna tattoos (to simulate tribal tattooing). Okay, some of the tattoos are real. They often dance in groups and have developed innovative cueing/signaling methods that allow groups to improvise in uniformity, giving the appearance of memorized choreography.

FUSION

As the name implies, it is not uncommon nowadays for dancers with multidisciplinary training to combine bellydance moves and costuming with other dance forms, such as flamenco, jazz, and Indian dance. Troupes such as Jillina and the Sahlala Dancers combine bellydance with extensive jazz training to produce Broadway-quality group dance numbers. Dalia Carella of New York has created her own style, Dunyavi Gypsy, based on her years of research into the gypsy roots of bellydance and costuming.

ABOVE: Carolena Nericcio, American tribal dance style

Chapter 3 | *Before We Begin*

A Short Glossary of Terminology Used in This Book

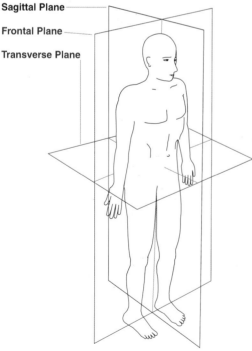

Sagittal Plane

Frontal Plane

Transverse Plane

The Planes of the Body

Movement of the human body is often described by the three planes that cross through or divide the body. The sagittal plane divides the body into left and right halves, the frontal plane divides it into front and back halves, and the transverse plane divides it into upper and lower halves. An understanding of these planes will help you understand movement descriptions such as those in this book. When practicing dance, it is helpful to visualize the plane in which each movement occurs.

Dance/Bellydance Terms

Arabesque [ar-a-besk]: A position of the body in which the dancer is standing on one leg and the other leg is extended to the back. In the case of Middle Eastern dance, an arabesque can also mean standing on one leg and lifting the other leg and hip straight up, with the foot in passé.

Demi-plié [dem-e-plee-ay]: A half-bending of the knees.

Demi-pointe: Standing on the balls of the feet. In everyday terms, we would refer to this position as being "on your toes." For trained dancers, being on their toes may mean en pointe, which is literally on the tips of their toes via toe shoes. Since we are not ballerinas, for the purpose of this book, we will use "on your toes," "in relevé," and "in demi-pointe" interchangeably.

Different names for bellydance: Raks Sharqi, Beledi, Middle Eastern dance, Oriental dance.

Grand plié: A full or complete bending of the knees.

Lock: A fast, sharp tensing of a given muscle group used as a percussive movement or accent movement in bellydance.

Passé [pa-say]: Lifting the foot to knee level or to pass it from the front to back.

Plié [plee-ay]: Bent, bending—a bending of the knee or knees

Relevé [ruhl-vay]: Raised—to raise the body onto half toe (demi-pointe).

The "Audience"

Since dance is made up of shapes and poses put together in a series, it is necessary to have a main focal point at which to present these shapes. Otherwise, if I say to make a circle with your right hip, and your right hip was facing the back wall, no one would see the wonderful circle you just created (including yourself, if you are practicing in the mirror). No one expects you to perform bellydance for an audience after reading this book, but for the sake of learning the movements and presenting them properly, we will use the terms "audience" and "facing front" loosely to describe the imaginary audience, the mirror, or the wall in front of you. It will help your form and visualization.

Chapter 4 | *Warm-Ups and Stretches*

Warming up and stretching muscles is recommended for any physical activity, to prevent injury, increase flexibility, and reduce soreness after a workout. Bellydancing works some smaller muscles that typically are not worked during normal day-to-day activity, such as the gluteus medius (posterior muscles around waist and hips), latissimus dorsi and trapezius (upper back muscles), and external obliques (sides), so it is important to warm up and stretch those specific muscles. Also, when one becomes an advanced dancer and performs most traveling steps in demi-pointe (on your toes), it is absolutely essential to incorporate a good calf warm-up and stretch to avoid muscle injury.

The following are basic bellydance movements that also serve as excellent warm-up exercises. You can find their step-by-step descriptions in the next two chapters.

Traditional Shimmy (p. 76)

Hip Slide (p. 66)

Hip Circle (p. 84)

Rib Slide (p. 59)

Ribs Forward and Back (p. 60)

Pelvic Tuck (p. 63)

Warm-Ups

A good warm-up should increase blood flow to the major muscle groups, thus "warming" the muscles and preparing them for activity. Usually, the extremities are warmed first, then (and most importantly) the erector spinae (muscles that run up and down the entire back or spine). Most injuries that occur due to lack of a proper warm-up occur in the muscles along the spine.

SHOULDER ROLLS

Warm up the shoulders by rolling them forward and backward.

GRAND PLIÉ

I always incorporate grand pliés into my warm-up routine because they are so effective at warming and working the entire leg. There are two ways to perform grand pliés: one is in first position, with the heels close to each other, and the other is second position, with the heels at least shoulder-width apart. If you have not had prior ballet training, I recommend the second position pliés, as they are less stressful to the ligaments of the knee.

1. Stand with feet shoulder-width apart, toes pointing out.

2. Bend the knees and lower the tailbone toward the floor.

3. As you lower into your plié, focus on leaning your weight back over your heels, as if you were about to sit down. (This puts the weight of the upper body in control of the muscles. If you were to lean forward, the ligaments of your knees would bear the weight of the upper body instead.) Make sure your knees are directly above your feet. If your knees are leaning more forward than your feet, widen your stance and plié again until the knees are directly over the feet. This position maximizes the warm-up of the muscles and minimizes stress on the knees.

4. Straighten the legs to return to standing position.

5. Repeat steps 1–4 for at least two sets of eight repetitions.

LATERAL LEG LIFTS

1. Stand with feet together.

2. Lift the right leg directly to the right side, pointing the toes. Lift only 6–12 inches, no more.

3. Hold briefly, then return to standing position.

4. Repeat on left side.

5. Alternate for at least two sets of eight repetitions.

Tip

Make sure you point the toes as you lift the leg. This will help warm up and strengthen the calves, feet, and ankles.

Plié with Arms

Let's maximize our warm-up by working the arms and legs simultaneously during pliés.

1. As you bend your knees into a plié, lower your arms laterally to waist level.

2. As you straighten your legs to return to a standing position, raise your arms laterally until they are overhead.

3. Repeat, repeat, repeat.

Variation

In addition to lifting and lowering arms during pliés, you can use a forward and backward motion to warm up the chest, shoulders, and back.

1. As you bend the knees into a plié, push your arms straight out in front of you (this will also help your balance as you lean your weight back during the plié).

2. As you straighten the legs to return to a standing position, pull the arms straight back, bending at the elbows. You should feel your shoulder blades squeeze together as you pull back.

3. Repeat.

Stretches

Never stretch a cold muscle! Never bounce into a stretch! Always warm up first, then stretch gently, relaxing into the stretch. These stretches can be performed before dancing (after warming up) and after dancing. Assuming you know some general stretches, here are some bellydance-specific stretches:

◄ BENT-KNEE HIP STRETCH

1. Stand with feet close together, both arms above head.

2. Bend the left knee and tilt both arms to the right, so entire left side of the body feels the stretch. Bending the left knee increases the stretch of the hip.

3. Hold position for several seconds, relaxing into stretch.

4. Repeat on other side.

Variation ▶

Instead of just bending the left leg as you lean to the right, cross the left leg behind you to maximize the stretch.

RIB CAGE STRETCH ▼

1. Clasp the hands behind the back and squeeze shoulder blades together, which pushes the rib cage forward.

2. If desired, tilt head back at the same time to maximize stretch.

3. With hands still clasped behind back, lean upper body forward and let the arms hang forward. Relax the neck and let the head hang. This will extend the stretch to the shoulders and the rhomboid muscles between the shoulder blades.

BACK AND SHOULDER STRETCH IN PLIÉ ▲

1. Stand with feet wide apart.

2. Bend into plié and rest hands on knees.

3. Lean right shoulder in and down toward floor in front of you. You should feel a stretch throughout the right shoulder and back.

4. Hold for several seconds, and relax into the stretch.

5. Repeat on the other side.

This is a wonderful stretch for the entire
back, and should be a regular part of
your fitness regimen.

Cat Position

This is the opposite of the Cow.

1. With palms and knees on the floor,
   and support in the abdominals, let your
   head hang down, looking at the floor.

2. Contract the back, assuming the position of a very angry cat. Try to imagine
   that you are pulling your belly button up
   to the ceiling, using your abdominals to
   help the back round out as much as
   possible. You should feel every muscle
   in your back being stretched.

3. Hold for five seconds.

4. Return to relaxed position.

Cow Position

1. With palms and knees on the floor, and support in the
   abdominals, arch your back and tilt your head up to look
   at the ceiling.

2. Hold for five seconds.

3. Return to relaxed position.

Repeat both Cat and Cow at least three times each.

KNEE-TO-CHEST ▲

1. Stand with feet shoulder-width apart.

2. Find your balance on left leg.

3. Bend the right knee and lift it to your chest. This will round out and stretch the lower back and glutei.

4. Repeat on other leg.

CALF STRETCH ▲

1. Stand with feet shoulder-width apart.

2. Bend knees slightly.

3. Lean forward, and rest both hands on right knee.

4. Put all your weight on right knee.

5. Extend the left leg out in front and point the toes to the ceiling.

6. Slowly increase lean forward to stretch left calf.

7. Repeat steps 1–6 on the other side.

◄ QUADRICEPS STRETCH

1. Stand with feet shoulder-width apart.

2. Find your balance on left leg.

3. Bend right leg behind you and grab right foot with right hand, pulling foot toward the body.

4. Hold position, relaxing into stretch.

5. Repeat on the other side.

Variation ►

Once you complete steps 1–4, you may wish to challenge yourself by leaning forward, which will further the stretch and develop your ability to balance on one leg.

CHIROPRACTOR STRETCH ►

I consider this stretch essential to bellydancing for its effectiveness in stretching the glutei, lower back, and hips. Even if you don't pursue bellydancing in the future, this is a great stretch, especially if you experience lower back stiffness.

1. Lie down on the floor with your back to the floor, arms and legs outstretched.

2. Bend the right leg and cross the right leg over the body, so right knee is facing left.

3. Keep the right arm and shoulder on the floor.

4. Relax and hold the stretch for at least five seconds.

5. Repeat with the other leg.

DON'T FORGET YOUR HANDS!

Bellydancing uses hand movements such as hand circles and hand undulations. Stretching the hands will increase flexibility and reduce stiffness. Nothing takes away from the beauty of a dance more than stiff, tense hands.

1. Grasp the fingertips and pull them back gently.

2. Hold for at least five seconds.

3. Then, grasp each finger separately and gently pull it back, one at a time.

4. Shake out the hands to get rid of tension in the hands and wrists.

NECK STRETCH

Perform these slowly and gently . . . the neck is very delicate!

1. Lean the head to the right gently, relaxing into the stretch.

2. Lean the head to the left.

3. Tilt head down as if looking down.

4. Look over right shoulder as far as you can.

Chapter 5 | *Fundamental Movements and Isolation Exercises*

Before practicing bellydance, always remember that almost all bellydance moves are performed with the feet together. One of my teachers used to tell me that my knees should be touching most of the time. This is for several reasons: a different set of muscles is used if the movements are done with legs in an open stance; the appearance of the moves will be completely different in an open stance (the most beautiful step can look vulgar if performed with the legs apart); having the feet together makes the hips appear more prominent, so even subtle hip movements will be noticeable; and most importantly, a closed stance keeps the hips centered over the body's center of gravity. Some people actually practice with their feet tied no more than six inches apart with a string, to learn good form.

Basic Hand/Arm Position

Hands and Arms

These hand and arm exercises work almost all the muscles in the hands, wrists, and arms, not just the major muscles. They work the muscles in a gentle way, toning them and improving grace and coordination. The hand exercises are great for anyone with repetitive motion syndrome (injuries that result from performing the same physical motion repeatedly, such as typing) because they work the muscles in the full range of motion.

Hand/arm position and gesture are essential to bellydancing. Many students focus too much on hip work and shimmies, but without correct and polished hand and arm movement, their dance will look amateurish. So, it's best to practice these movements from the very beginning.

BASIC HAND/ARM POSITION

For reference, let's remember the basic hand and arm position for bellydance. Most hand and arm movements will start at this position (see opposite page). Also, any bellydance moves or combinations can be performed with hands and arms at this position.

Arms should be at sides with slight bend in the elbow, slight break at the wrist, fingers straight and together, with palms facing the floor. The upper arm and elbow should not be touching the sides of the body, as this is incorrect form and hides the movement of the body. Always keep enough room for air flow between sides of the body and arms/elbows.

HAND CIRCLES

Hold your hands with your fingers straight and together. The thumb should be tucked into the palm so that it aligns with the middle finger. For the sake of describing this exercise, let's pretend the tip of your middle finger is a pencil.

1. Draw a circle in the air with your pencil, moving clockwise.

2. Repeat for one set of eight circles, then change direction to counterclockwise and do another set of eight.

SNAKE ARMS

The concept here is that the entire arm will undulate in a snake-like way (hence the name). It is important to remember that all the movement from the arms will occur in the frontal plane, meaning along the sides of the body, without any part of the arm or hand moving toward the front or back of the body.

Benefit: This exercise develops arm strength and coordination. It stretches and strengthens all the muscles from the shoulders to the wrist.

1. Start in the Basic Arm Position.

2. Lift the right shoulder and rotate forward slightly. This will make your elbow turn to face the ceiling.

3. Lift the right elbow up toward the ceiling, so that the elbow is

higher than the shoulder or wrist. The arm should have a curve as the elbow lifts, as if you are holding and lifting a beach ball against the side of your body.

4. Lift the wrist so that the wrist is higher toward the ceiling than the shoulder or elbow, and drop the elbow so that the elbow is much lower than the shoulder or wrist (drop the beach ball).

5. Repeat so the movement is fluid and undulating. Keep repeating above steps, lifting the shoulder, elbow, then wrist, as if you are lifting and dropping a beach ball.

6. Once you master the steps above, perform the movement so that when one elbow is at its highest point toward the ceiling, the other elbow is at its lowest point toward the floor. Both arms perform the same movement, but in opposite directions from each other (one arm is dropping the beach ball while the other is lifting the beach ball).

7. Repeat steps 1-6, creating resistance for your arms at all phases of this exercise, so that the movement looks like you are moving your arms while they are suspended in a thick liquid.

    Creating resistance for yourself will not only give the movement the correct look, but it will also ensure that you are working all the muscles involved in the movement, including the supporting muscles.

    You should feel all the muscles in your arms and shoulders working. This exercise may seem awkward at first (as will most new exercises), but with practice, your snake arms will be smooth and effortless. Practice, practice, practice!

Variation

Snake Arms can be performed as above, or directly in front of the body.

4

HANDS CROSS AND UNCROSS ▲

1. Start with hands/arms in basic position.

2. Move hands to the front of the body and cross one hand over the other, palms still facing down.

3. Turn hands so they are in the same crossed position, only now the palms are facing up toward the ceiling.

4. Move hands back to sides, then flip palms down so you are back to basic position.

◄ SWAY ARMS

Similar to Snake Arms, but the arms move in front of the body from side to side (in the transverse plane), and they do not oppose each other.

1. Both elbows, then the wrists move to the right.

2. Both elbows, then wrists move to the left.

Tip

Imagine you are standing waist-high in water, and you are swishing your hands across the surface of the water.

Variation

This move can also be performed higher up (at shoulder level) or overhead (in the frontal plane).

HANDS CROSSED ON ASCENT, OPEN ON DESCENT ▾

This movement can be done as a move by itself, or layered over a
Hip Shimmy.

1. Start with hands/arms in basic position.

2. Move hands to the front of the body and cross one hand over the other,
   palms still facing down.

3. Keeping hands crossed at the wrist, lift the elbows, so the hands are in
   the same position, but lower than the elbows. Continue to lift elbows so
   that the crossed hands end up framing the head.

4. Slowly uncross the hands, opening up the arms with palms facing up as
   you bring the arms back down the sides of the body toward the starting
   position.

5. When your arms reach the basic position, flip the wrists so the palms are
   facing down again.

6. Repeat steps 1–5, creating resistance for your arms at all phases of this
   exercise.

4

1   2   3

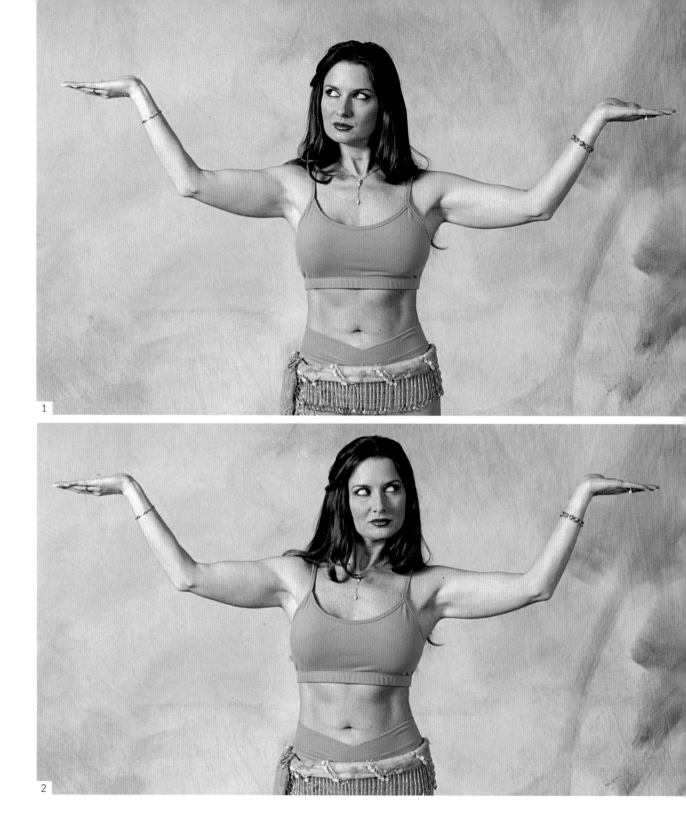

1

2

Head, Neck, and Shoulders

There are only a few basic movements of the head and neck, but they are important for isolating the muscles in the neck from the muscles in the shoulders. I find the head and neck exercises particularly interesting, since the neck is an often-neglected part of the body. Since so many people store tension in their neck and shoulders, these exercises are wonderful. They also help prevent sagging and wrinkling of the neck.

Important: Always perform exercises of the neck very gently. Never throw the head around or use force. These exercises employ just a gentle leaning of the head and neck.

◀ HEAD SLIDES

To perform head slides and head circles, it is important to understand that the head does not actually move; it is the neck that moves. The following visualization tool may seem funny, but it works, so here goes: remember the Frankenstein Monster? Remember those bolts he had sticking out of the sides of his neck? Okay, now imagine you have those bolts, and someone pulls them left and right, making your neck go back and forth. Your head just happens to be on top of your neck, so it will follow.

Benefit: Strengthens, tones, and improves control and flexibility of the neck muscles.

1. To slide the head to the right, move the neck directly out to the right without moving your shoulders. Make sure you do not tilt your head sideways; keep it straight.

2. Now slide the head to the left by moving the neck to the left keeping your shoulders steady.

So, the head is staying straight the whole time; it just appears to be sliding back and forth along an imaginary line.

Variations

You can pose your hands near the head to help showcase or frame the movement of the head. As your head slides right and left, the hands stay still. For example, you can:

1. Hold both hands straight with palms down under the chin, like a shelf.

2. Hold one hand under and one over the head, as though the head were between two shelves.

3. Hold both hands flat, palms facing up, next to the head at ear level (Pharaonic style). Or try head circles.

4. Head Circles

   a. Let's take the Head Slide a step further by making the head slide to the front and back.

   b. Next, try sliding the head to the right, front, left, then back.

   c. Repeat until the movement is smooth and circular.

Tips for Head Circle

Imagine that you have a pencil pointing up from the top of your head, and you are drawing a circle on the ceiling. Remember, the head does not tilt sideways at any time; you should be able to perform this exercise with a book balanced on your head.

1

KHALEEGY HAIR TOSS ▲

This is just one move from the Khaleegy (pronounced kha-lee-jee) folkloric dance style. Many bellydancers incorporate Khaleegy movements into their bellydance routines. It may help to know that this movement originated in the Arabian Gulf (Khaleegy) region, where it is customary for women to grow their hair as long as possible. This dance movement is actually meant to show off the beauty of the hair by tossing it from side to side, so the hair becomes part of the dance. When done properly, it is a very beautiful movement to watch.

Benefit: Gently stretches the neck muscles.

1. Make sure neck and shoulders are relaxed and warmed up.

2. Tilt the head toward the right shoulder, so your eyes are looking up at the left ceiling corner, and your right ear is close to your right shoulder.

3. Gently swing the head around the back, so that you end up with the head leaning to the left, with your eyes looking up to the right ceiling corner.

Basically, you have the starting and ending positions of the head tilted on each side, and in order to get from point A to point B, you lean your head slightly back and toss your hair.

Variation: Figure Eight of the Head

Similar to the Hair Toss, but with an extra step.

1. Lean head to the right, so your eyes are looking up at the left ceiling corner and your right ear is close to your right shoulder.

2. Lean head directly back, so you are looking up.

3. Return head to upright, normal position.

4. Lean head to the left, with eyes looking up at the right ceiling corner.

5. Lean head directly back, so you are looking up.

6. Return head to upright, normal position.

So, if we had our imaginary pencil pointing up out of the top of our head, we would be drawing a figure eight.

2

ZAR HEAD ROLL ▲

There is a famous head movement that originates from an ancient trance/exorcism dance known as the Zar. This movement was performed repeatedly until the person fell into a trance. The same movement is also sometimes used in Khaleegy dance, but only one or two repetitions at a time are thrown in with other steps.

Although I will describe the movement here because it is popular and has become a standard used in bellydance, I must caution against performing this move repeatedly, since it is unhealthy for the bones of the neck. It is fine to perform it slowly to relax and stretch the neck muscles, but not quickly as in the original dance. The most I would recommend anyone performing this movement is two or three times. Execute it

slowly, in a relaxed fashion, then move on to something else, unless you have specifically trained for the Zar dance for a very long time. The movement involves the circumduction of the neck, which the bones of the neck were not intended to do.

To perform a Zar head roll:

1. *Gently* tilt head to the right, then back, then left, then front, so that the head is making a full circle.

2. Repeat several times. *Gently*.

2 3

Tips

Make sure, only the shoulders are moving.
The movement should look loose and relaxed.
If you perform this movement in the mirror
and it looks stiff or jerky, make sure to breathe
and focus on relaxing the entire body.

SHOULDER SHIMMY ▲

Shoulder Shimmies are great exercise for the deltoid (shoulder) muscles. They are also great for teaching you how to separate your shoulder muscles from your neck muscles. Many people have so much stiffness in their neck and shoulders that all the muscles in that region move like one big, stiff muscle. Isolating and gently working these muscles will relieve tension and improve posture and flexibility.

1. Start in the Basic Position.

2. Lean the right shoulder forward, without moving the arms, hands, or neck.

3. Lean the left shoulder forward as the right returns to normal position.

4. Repeat over and over again, right, left, right, left, and so on, gaining speed.

Ribs, Upper Abdominals, Obliques, and Upper Back

RIB SLIDES ▾

Benefit: This exercise works the upper abdominals and oblique muscles, both in terms of toning and shaping.

1. Stand with hands on hips.

2. Lean rib cage directly out to the right. You should feel a stretch in the muscles on your left side.

3. Repeat on the left side by sliding ribs to the left.

4. Repeat side to side until the movement is smooth.

3

2

RIBS FORWARD AND BACK ▾

Benefit: Stretches and strengthens the upper abdominals, rhomboids (between the shoulder blades in back), and erector spinae (back).

Same as the Rib Slide but in the sagittal plane, so the rib cage moves forward, then back. This movement is excellent for stretching, relieving tension, and strengthening the muscles in the upper back.

2

1

1. Move the rib cage forward. You should feel your shoulder blades squeeze together slightly as they help to push the chest forward.

2. Move the ribs toward the back. You should feel the shoulder blades separate slightly as the rib cage pushes to the back.

2. Drop the chest back to normal position. When you drop the chest, make sure the shoulders don't start to lean forward. Dropping the chest is simply returning it to its original position.

3. Repeat the lift-drop sequence for at least two sets of eight repetitions.

You should feel your upper abdominal muscles working to help lift the chest. This movement is great for building definition of the upper abdominal muscles.

A more advanced version of this movement would involve the lifting and dropping of the chest repeatedly with such speed that it is considered a Chest Shimmy. This is an extremely difficult movement that originates from African dance.

CHEST LIFTS AND DROPS ▲

Benefit: Stretches and strengthens the upper abdominals, rhomboids (between the shoulder blades), and erector spinae (back).

1. Standing with hands on hips, lift the chest upward, making sure nothing else moves except the chest (watch out for your shoulders; they will want to move).

RIB CIRCLE IN THE FRONTAL PLANE ▶

Benefit: *Works the upper abdominals and obliques.*

Now let's imagine we have a pencil pointing out from our chest.

1. Slide the ribs to the right.

2. Lift the chest up.

3. Slide the ribs to the left.

4. Drop the chest back to center.

5. Repeat the sequence of right, up, left, and down until it becomes a smooth circle.

Do at least sixteen moving clockwise, then change direction and move counterclockwise.

Tip
Imagine you have a pencil pointing out from the front of your chest. While doing Rib Circles, your pencil should draw a complete circle on the mirror in front of you. You are practicing in front of a mirror, aren't you?

Variation
Rib Circle in the Sagittal Plane
Same concept as the Rib Circle in the Frontal Plane, except that the chest slides out to the front, then lifts up, then slides to the back, then returns to center. Repeat front, up, back, and center, like a Ferris wheel.

Benefit: Works the upper abdominals and rhomboids.

Abdominals, Lower Back, and Hips ▶

PELVIC TUCK

Benefit: Works the lower abdominals and buttocks.

1. Stand with feet together, knees slightly bent.

2. Concentrate on pulling in the lower abdominals, such that the pelvis tucks underneath the body.

3. Release to relaxed standing position, then repeat.

Tip

Do this facing your profile to a mirror so you can see if you are performing this movement correctly. When the lower abdominals are flexed and the pelvis tucks under the body, the spine should round out at the lower back. In other words, the normal curve of the lower back will disappear while the pelvis is tucked, and return when the pelvis is returned to the normal, relaxed position. This will warm up the lower abdominals and lower lumbar spine, and will also add strength and flexibility to both the lower abdominals and lower back. Aside from the physical benefits, this is a key movement in bellydancing, as it is the basis for executing many other essential bellydance steps, such as the Camel.

1   2

PELVIC CAMEL ▲

Benefit: Works the lower abdominals, lower back, and buttocks.

This movement is one step further from the Pelvic Tuck.

1. Begin by pulling in lower abdominals and tucking the pelvis, but bend the knees.

2. Now, straighten both knees as you push the pelvis forward, so that you are standing straight up and your hips are leaning forward.

3. Repeat the first two steps until the movement looks fluid and undulating. Tuck the pelvis, move the hips back and down as you bend the knees.

4. Push the hips up and forward as you straighten the knees.

The front-and-back movement of the hips, combined with the up-and-down level change from bending and straightening the knees, gives this movement a figure eight shape.

3

4

1

◄ HIP SLIDE

Benefit: Stretches and develops control in the sides of the hips and outer thighs.

1. Standing with feet together, gently lean right hip only directly out to the right (not up or down), such that the right hip is farther out to the right than any other body part.

2. Repeat with the left hip, then alternate left and right until the movement is smooth.

2

THE BELLY ROLL ▶

Some call it a Belly Wave, some call it a Belly Roll. This exercise originated thousands of years ago as preparation for childbirth, both in terms of helping with contractions during labor, and giving muscles the elasticity and strength to recover after giving birth.

Benefit: The Belly Roll works wonders for gaining control of all the individual muscles that make up the abdominal region. It's only logical that if you can control and exercise these muscles separately, you will have greater definition in the abdominal region.

It can take months to learn how to do a Belly Roll, so please be patient. It took me three months to learn, and I practiced daily.

If you look at my abdomen, you will notice that although my stomach muscles are clearly defined, they are not quite as rock hard and chiseled-looking as those of some athletes who train their abs only to tighten. The look is defined with a bit of softness. This is because my abdominal muscles are stretched outward in addition to being tightened.

Let's begin by learning how to pull the stomach in and push it out. It may seem awkward to push the stomach out at first, but think about it: how healthy can it be to only tighten these muscles?

Part 1: Basic Push and Pull

To push the stomach out:

1. Inhale, letting the air push out your diaphragm, which makes your stomach expand (make sure you are not expanding the rib cage; only the stomach).

2. Concentrate on pushing your stomach out at the same time, like when you were a kid and you tried to imitate a pregnant woman.

Tip

This may take a lot of practice. It is important to inhale during this phase, and to really make sure the diaphragm, not the rib cage, is expanding. (Note: this same exercise is also taught by vocal instructors to improve control of the diaphragm.)

To pull the stomach in:

1. Stand sideways looking into a mirror (you really do need a mirror for this).

2. Without leaning the shoulders forward or moving any other body part, squeeze the stomach muscles in as tight and as far back into the body as they can go, letting all the air out of your lungs.

3. Hold for five seconds. Release.

Practice steps 1–3, at least thirty repetitions per day, until you can see a big difference between the Push and Pull positions. You should be able to pull your stomach in, and push it out, farther than ever before.

Tips

Although this exercise is just the foundation for the Belly Roll, it is by itself a great abdominal workout that can easily be done anywhere (even while driving), since you don't have to lie on the floor as with a conventional sit-up. As long as you really squeeze the abdominals when you pull them in, and hold for a few seconds, you will have an effective sculpting exercise by this movement alone. Once you are good at this part, move on to the next exercise.

Part 2: Top In and Out, Bottom In and Out

1. Inhale and only push out the upper abdominals. You can physically hold your lower abdominals in with your hands if it helps, but you must focus your mind on controlling the upper abdominals separately from the lower abdominals.

2. Repeat for about two sets of eight repetitions.

3. Push the lower abdominals out further than the upper abdominals. Obviously, we don't push the lower abdominals out by filling them with air, so we must use a different method to push the lower abdominals than the upper. Hold in the upper abdominals by keeping them in a relaxed but supported position. Now, let the lower abdominals relax so that they just sort of hang out.

4. Next, gently squeeze the muscle back to a relaxed but supported position. Repeat for about two sets of eight repetitions.

It may take a few weeks to develop strength and coordination between the upper and lower abdominals. Once you are able to control your upper and lower abdominals with your mind, move on to the next step toward being a champion belly roller.

Part 3: Top Out Bottom In, Bottom Out Top In ▶

1. Start with the upper abdominals pushed out and the lower abs pulled in.

2. Switch positions, so the lower abs are pushed out and the upper abs pulled in.

3. Repeat these two steps in the mirror until you can do them consistently by just commanding your body to do so. (At this point, you should not have to rely on inhaling and exhaling to control the diaphragm; your muscles should be able to move on their own.)

Part 4: The Final Step

Now that you have sufficient abdominal control, the Belly Roll can be performed either of two ways (or both, if you are feeling ambitious).

Method One

1. Push the entire stomach out.

2. Pull in the bottom only.

3. Then pull in the top as you release the bottom.

4. Repeat steps 1–3 smoothly in succession.

Method Two

1. Start with the entire stomach pulled in as far as it can be.

2. Push the top out.

3. Push the bottom out while pulling the top back in.

4. Repeat steps 1–3 smoothly in succession.

Pick which method works best for you, and enjoy your newfound belly rolling skill. Aside from the physical benefits, it's great for impressing people at parties and entertaining small children.

THE SIDEWAYS BELLY ROLL

Although it is rare to see a bellydancer who has mastered the Sideways Belly Roll, it is certainly worth mentioning. I perform this movement, and I was inspired by a dancer from Southern California named Fahtiem, who is a master at stomach movements, particularly this one.

After having mastered controlling the upper and lower abdominals, the next step is to divide the stomach into left and right sections. The same principals and steps apply as with the Belly Roll, but we are going from side to side.

1. Start out by pushing the left side out and the right in.

2. Then push the right side out while holding the left side in.

3. Repeat the movements in steps 1–2 until you have a fluid and undulating lateral movement. I make it sound simple, but it requires months of practice and much concentration. Don't let that be a deterrent.

THE BELLY FLUTTER

The Flutter is the equivalent of a shimmy of the belly. It simply involves pushing the diaphragm out and in repeatedly, but very rapidly.

1. First, most of the air is emptied from the lungs, as the movement occurs faster than the lungs can fill with and release air.

2. Then, push the diaphragm out and in quickly.

Since there is no breathing during this exercise, most dancers only do flutters for a few seconds. Try doing five in a row. Then gradually increase the amount of repetitions. Fifteen is a good number to be able to do at one time, but the sky is the limit.

Legs and Feet

Here is a simple drill that exercises the legs and feet, and will help your legs and feet have correct form in your dancing.

1. Stand with feet together, flat on the floor, with good posture in the entire body.

2. Brush the right foot forward slightly while pointing the toe. When the leg brushes forward, think about the movement being controlled by the inner thigh muscle pulling the leg forward. All the muscles in your leg and foot should be engaged to support the straight leg position and pointed toe.

Tip

A common mistake many students make when first learning bellydance is that they focus so much on the hip isolations, they forget about practicing good form of the hands and feet. The end result looks sloppy, unprofessional, and sometimes vulgar. I recommend practicing all bellydance exercises in front of a mirror, and with every hip or stomach isolation you practice, check your hand, arm, and foot positions. If you are doing fantastic Belly Rolls but you are standing pigeon-toed, the audience will focus on your feet, not your Belly Rolls. Elements of your dancing that are incorrect will stand out more than those that are correct, because they look out of place.

3. Brush the foot, toe still pointed, so the leg moves in an arc along the floor to the side of the body. This movement should come from the muscle of the outer thigh (abductor).

4. Toe still pointed, brush the foot in an arc along the floor to the back.

5. Return the foot to starting position, with both feet flat on the floor.

6. Repeat this sequence at least sixteen times on each leg, always checking your form in the mirror to ensure a straight leg and pointed toe.

4

3

The Face

Yes, the face. Although we will not be exercising the face, we must make it a point to learn how to relax the face. Literally command your facial muscles to relax. Bellydancing is not easy, but no one really wants to see that in your face. Your audience will enjoy watching you if you look as though you are enjoying yourself. They will feel uncomfortable watching you if you look like you are in pain. It is a very big part of the dance to have a relaxed, smiling, and subtly flirtatious expression on the face. This is one of the most important aspects of the dance, and unfortunately, it frequently gets over-looked in the classroom. I have found that learning to relax my face has helped reduce tension in my face throughout all areas of my life, not just when dancing. Good-bye tension headaches! Good-bye frown lines!

Chapter 6 | *Basic Bellydance Steps*

Shimmies, Ommis, and Locks

Shimmies are the fast, percussive shaking and vibrating movements of the hips that everyone expects a bellydancer to be doing. Two important factors in all shimmies are keeping the feet together and keeping support in the abdominals so that the pelvis does not extend out to the back, away from the center of gravity.

Benefit: Aside from developing rhythm and control, the various shimmies improve circulation and release tension from all areas of the body.

TRADITIONAL SHIMMY ▼

This is the original shimmy as it has been performed for thousands of years, and is sometimes referred to as the Old Style Shimmy.

1. Standing with feet together and knees ever-so-slightly bent, gently bend the right knee so that the right hip drops just a bit.

2. Repeat left. As the left hip drops, the right returns to normal position.

3. Keep repeating the above, simply alternating the bending and straightening of the knees, which facilitates the bouncing of the hips.

◄ EGYPTIAN SHIMMY

This is a newer shimmy, developed during the 1940s and 1950s as the Egyptian cinema was experiencing a golden age. Much care was taken to refine the dance form, which was previously largely based on folkloric dance. Costumes were designed with elegance, and traditional bellydance steps were taken to a new level by adding some Western influences, such as ballet.

So, the Traditional Shimmy, which is traditionally performed in demi-plié (knees slightly bent), is now modified to be performed with straight legs.

1

2

Tip

Most students wear a hip scarf around their hips that is decorated with coins and beads. The sound of the coins and beads rattling with the hip movement will let you know if your hips are moving in time with the music.

1

Variation: Choo Choo ▲

Same as an Egyptian Shimmy, but performed in demi-pointe. Once you are standing in demi-pointe and shimmying by alternating the knees, you will notice a natural tendency of the body to start to travel forward. Continue traveling forward while shimmying, making sure that the shimmy comes from bending and straightening the knees, not from the stepping of the feet. Make sure to keep the tension out of the legs, as it will change the movement. If you feel you are tensing up, take a deep breath and focus on relaxing all the muscles and making the shimmy movement come from the bending of the knees.

2

BOUNCE SHIMMY ▼

This movement is basically the same as the Egyptian Shimmy, except that the knees do not alternate bending, they bend at the same time. Subsequently, the movement is much larger and a bit slower.

1. Stand with both feet together and legs straight.

2. Simply bend both knees slightly.

3. Straighten both knees again, so that your body bounces.

Repeat the above bending and straightening of both knees simultaneously, keeping time with the music. Keep your heels on the floor, and just focus on repeatedly bending and straightening both knees together in time with the music, remembering to relax the body and face. This is probably the easiest of shimmies.

TWIST SHIMMY ▶

This movement is similar to the Egyptian Shimmy, except that the knees not only bend slightly, they lean in toward the opposite leg at the same time. The appearance of the movement is a shimmy with a slight front-to-back twist, due to the angling of the knee. Because of the addition of the twist, it is a slower shimmy than the Traditional Shimmy and the Egyptian Shimmy. It also engages the outer thigh muscles, as opposed to the other shimmies, which work the front and back of the legs.

VIBRATION SHIMMY

Throughout each description of the various shimmies, I have been telling you how important it is to relax while shimmying, and that if you start to become tense, slow down, take a deep breath, and relax.

Well, in a nutshell, a Vibration Shimmy is a very tense version of a Traditional Shimmy. Because the body is tense during this shimmy, the shaking movement is smaller and less visible from a distance.

The Skinny on Shimmies

So what's the difference between the Traditional Shimmy and the Egyptian Shimmy? There is a big difference in what may seem to be a subtle distinction between the two. Since the knees are always bent during the Traditional Shimmy, the muscles of the legs must support the weight of the upper body, which can make you tire rather quickly. Also, while your leg muscles are supporting the weight of the body and moving the knees to create the shimmy, they are somewhat tense, as they are completely engaged.

During an Egyptian Shimmy, the weight of the upper body is supported by the skeletal system rather than the muscles of the legs, because the legs are straight. Take the hip movement out of the equation completely, if you will, and consider how much easier it is to stand with your legs straight, as you would normally stand, as opposed to standing with both knees bent. With an Egyptian Shimmy, the large muscle groups in the legs are relaxed, and only the small muscle behind the knees works to slightly bend the knee and bring it back to standing position. Thus, it is easier to perform an Egyptian Shimmy for longer intervals.

◀ THE OMMI

Ommis are wonderful and popular movements that combine the hip shimmy and the pelvic tilt. They are somewhat similar to a Hip Circle, but the up-and-down tilting of the pelvis adds another dimension, so the hips look like they are doing more of a gyration than a circle.

Benefit: Improved strength, flexibility, and control of the pelvic region, including buttocks and lower abdominals.

Variations: Smooth Ommi versus Segmented Ommi

The Ommi as described above is considered a Segmented Ommi, since each phase of the Ommi is performed sharply and clearly with each beat.

The movement can also be performed by smoothly cycling through all the steps so the hips are changing positions without stopping, as though they are circling around the body.

3

4

Variation: Locks

Each phase of the Segmented Ommi can be used independently, and in that case would be referred to as a Hip Lock. Locks are often used as accent moves. For example, during a count of four, you could shimmy for the counts 1–3, then Lock the right hip on the fourth beat. Shimmy again for counts 1–3, then Lock the left hip, and so on.

1. Stand with your feet close together. Bend the left knee only, so that the right hip is pushed out to the right side.

2. Straighten both legs and pull in the lower abdominals so the pelvis tucks underneath you.

3. Bend the right knee so that the left hip pushes out to the left side.

4. Bend both knees so that the pelvis is no longer tucked.

5. Repeat the above steps sequentially to the music, so that you are continually changing the position of the hips right, tuck, left, untuck. Do one position for each beat.

Tip

One of the most important things to remember is to pull in the lower abdominals during the pelvic tuck phase. It really helps give the movement proper form.

Basic Bellydance Steps ✳ **83**

Circles and Figure Eights

HIP CIRCLE (Horizontal) ▶

Benefit: This movement is excellent for stretching, strengthening, and increasing flexibility to the gluteus medius, lower back, and illiopsoas (hip flexor) muscles.

1. Standing with feet together, gently lean right hip only directly out to the right (not up or down), without moving the feet or bending the knees, such that the right hip is leaning farther out to the right than any other body part.

2. Lean both hips forward, so that the hips are farther out in front than any other body part.

3. Next, slide or lean the hips to the left.

4. Finally, lean hips to the back, so they are farther out in back than any other body part. Pulling in your lower abdominals will help facilitate this movement.

5. Keep repeating the above steps, leaning the hips right, forward, left, then back. When you are warmed up with the movement, try smoothing it out, so that instead of hitting all four directions separately, your hips are making one big circle around the body, like a hula hoop. So, if we had imaginary pencils pointing downward from each hip, we would be drawing a giant circle on the ground.

1

2

3

4

Variation: Big Hip Circle ▼

Same as the Hip Circle, but really big. You are still leaning the hips front, right, back, left, and so on, but you exaggerate the leaning as far as possible away from the body. The movement should be so big that when you lean your hips to the back, they go back so far that you have to lean your upper body forward to keep balance. Think big.

Big Hip Circle

Basic Bellydance Steps ✳ **85**

1   2

VERTICAL HIP CIRCLE ▲

A Vertical Hip Circle is done only on one hip. It really helps to visualize making the shape of a circle during this movement. This movement looks great performed slowly and sensually, or playfully at a medium tempo.

Benefit: Sculpts the waistline.

Start by keeping your weight on one leg (let's say the right leg for this example). Point the left foot so that your posture is the same as if you are going to do a Hip Drop. Instead of dropping the hip, follow these steps.

1. Lift the left hip by keeping the left foot pointed and straightening the left knee.

2. Drop the left hip by bending the knee, and lean it toward the front at the same time.

3. Keeping the hip dropped, lean it toward the back.

4. Keeping the hip in back, lift the hip by straightening the knee.

5. Return to the lifted position of step 1 and repeat, making a smooth circle.

◄ HORIZONTAL FIGURE EIGHT

Similar in concept to the Hip Circle, the Horizontal Figure Eight is sort of a mini–Hip Circle on each hip, instead of one big one. Your hips will literally make the shape of a number 8, or infinity symbol. It is also strictly a movement within the transverse plane. Let's go through the steps.

Tips

If we had our imaginary pencil pointing down from each hip, each hip would be drawing its own circle on the floor. It is very important to keep your feet and legs close together. This will accentuate the hip movement.

1

2 3

4   5

6

1. Lean the right hip diagonally out in front. Not directly in front, not directly to the right, but rather, lean the right hip toward the front right corner.

2. Next, lean the right hip directly out to the right side.

3. Lean the right hip directly to the back.

4. Return right hip to center.

5. Repeat steps 1–4 with the left hip.

6. Keep repeating steps 1–5 so that the hips alternate making a smooth circle.

Benefit: This movement develops strength and flexibility in the hips and lower abdominals. Although we don't actually use the lower abdominal muscles to perform the steps 1–5, when you begin repeating the movements, you will be relying on lower abdominals to help switch from one hip to another. You'll feel it.

Variations

The Horizontal Figure Eight is a very versatile move. It can be performed slowly and seductively, or quickly (almost as fast as a shimmy) and livelily. It can be done with either straight legs, or in plié. You can also travel, walking either forward or back while your hips are making a figure eight. Here's how:

Each time the right hip leans diagonally forward to start the movement, take a small step with the right foot. Each time the left hip leans diagonally forward, step with the left foot, thus alternating the step/circle on each hip. Take small steps so that your feet are still close together. Try it!

VERTICAL FIGURE EIGHT ▶

This is the same concept as a Horizontal Figure Eight, except that it is entirely in the frontal plane. Let's go through the steps.

Benefit: Sculpts and trims the sides of the waist.

1. Stand with feet together, and good posture.

2. Point the right toe so that the right hip is lifted.

3. Lean the right hip out to the right, so it is farther right than any other part of the body.

4. Drop the right heel to the ground, so the right foot is flat and the right hip is lowered.

5. Return the right hip to normal, centered position.

6. Repeat steps 2–5 on the left hip.

1

2   3

4

- *Both Horizontal and Vertical Figure Eights can start from the opposite direction as that described here. For example, the Horizontal Figure Eight can start from the back right diagonal, then to the side, then front and back to center.*

- *The Vertical Figure Eight can also start by first dropping the hip, then to the side, then lifting the hip, then back to center, which is the opposite of our example.*

- *You can perform the same Vertical Figure Eight without lifting your heels off the ground to make the hip lift. Simply keep both feet flat on the ground, with knees slightly bent as your starting posture. Instead of pointing the toe in step 2 to lift the hip, just lift and drop the hip by bending and straightening your knee. Although it is a bit easier to do this movement by lifting the heels, there may be times when you want the focus to be strictly on the hips.*

- *You can also apply the same horizontal and vertical figure-eight movements to the rib cage.*

Continue alternating hip up, to the side, then down/back to center on each hip, making the movement smooth and rhythmic. Think of our imaginary pencils pointing directly forward, as if they are sticking out of our hip bones in the front. Each hip would be alternating drawing a circle on the wall in front of us.

1   2

Tips

The leg that belongs to the dropping hip should be facing directly in front; one of the biggest mistakes people make when learning this movement is to lean the knee out. The hands should be in the basic arm position, with the right arm straight and pointing down and the left pointing up to the ceiling, so the right arm is framing the hip. Keep support in the lower abdominals and pelvis tucked.

Once you are comfortable with the movement on both sides, try alternating from right to left in time with the music. Here's how: Count along with the music—1, 2, 3, 4, and so on. Drop the right hip on the 1, 2, and 3, but on 4, instead of dropping the hip, do the transition, so that the left hip is ready to drop on the next count of 1. Repeat on the left and continue alternating.

Hip Drops and Lifts

HIP DROP ▲

This movement is one of the most important moves in bellydance.

Benefit: Works the hips and illiopsoas muscles, and increases flexibility in the hips.

1. Standing with feet together, point right toe and lift right hip.

2. With right toe still pointed, bend right knee and drop right hip.

3. Repeat steps 1 and 2, lifting and dropping the hip repeatedly to the beat. The toe stays pointed the entire time.

4. After at least three sets of eight drops, transition to the left hip. See "Transitioning Right and Left Hip Drops"

THE HIP LIFT

Remember that when doing a Hip Drop, we made the Hip Drop on the beat. The mechanics of the Hip Lift are the same as the Hip Drop, where one toe is pointed and that knee straightens and bends to lift and drop the hip. The only difference is that with the Hip Lift, the hip will lift on the beat, so the lifting is the accent instead of the dropping.

Variations

1. You can vary your arm positioning to get different looks for your Hip Drop with diagonal arms, hands in hair, one hand at forehead, one in basic position.

2. You can make your Hip Drops lean forward or back by leaning the knee toward the inside or outside of the body, respectively. It is common to alternate Hip Drops to the front and back on counts 1 and 2, or try alternating front, center, back, center on counts 1, 2, 3, 4.

Transitioning Right and Left Hip Drops

The best way to transition from the right Hip Drop to the left is simply to stay in the same position, and change positions of the feet. Standing in the position for a right Hip Drop, with the right toe pointed and left flat:

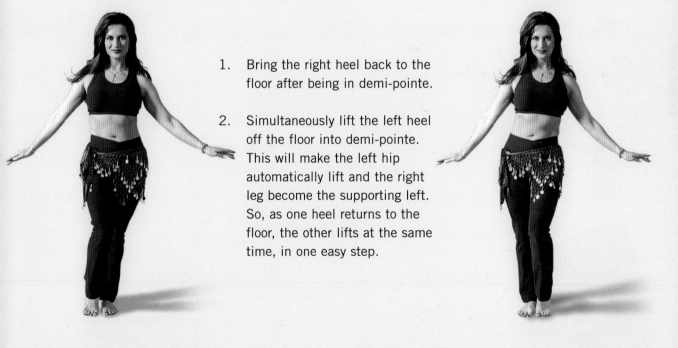

1. Bring the right heel back to the floor after being in demi-pointe.

2. Simultaneously lift the left heel off the floor into demi-pointe. This will make the left hip automatically lift and the right leg become the supporting left. So, as one heel returns to the floor, the other lifts at the same time, in one easy step.

DROP AND KICK ▶

Here is another bellydance must-have step for your dance vocabulary. The Drop and Kick is a variation of the Hip Drop, where you alternate dropping the hip two different ways.

Benefit: Works the hips, illiopsoas muscles, and thighs, and increases flexibility in the hips.

We learned how to drop the hip by pointing one toe and bending the knee. Here's another way to drop the hip, the Kick:

1. Instead of bending the knee to drop the hip, keep the leg completely straight, toe pointed, and drop the hip by letting your foot slide in front of you, like a little, delicate kick.

2. Practice lifting the hip, and dropping the hip by brushing the foot slightly along the floor in front of you. Practice this to music, and be sure to practice in front of a mirror. The hip movement should look the same as in the Hip Drop, with the only difference being that the brushing of the foot is the cause of the hip dropping, as opposed to the bending of the knee.

Tip

When you are ready to try alternating from right hip to left hip, use the same transition as with the Hip Drop. For example, you might try two Drop and Kicks, which are two counts each, for a total of four beats. Before the first beat of the next measure, do the transition, and on the next count of 1, begin the Drop and Kick on the other hip for the next four beats.

1

2

Variation

You can drop the hip just by using the kick method repeatedly, for a completely different look.

3

Now that you have the Kick part down to a science, let's alternate dropping the hip by bending the knee with dropping the hip by brushing the foot (the Drop and Kick).

1. Start from the same positions as the Hip Drop, with the right toe pointed and right hip lifted. Left leg is straight, left foot flat on the floor.

2. Drop the right hip by bending the right knee.

3. Lift the right hip by straightening the right knee.

4. Drop the right hip by brushing (kicking) the right foot in front of you. (Remember to keep the toe pointed when you brush.)

4

5. Lift the right hip by bringing the right foot back to its original position, as in step 1.

6. Repeat the drop, lift, kick, lift pattern until you can do it smoothly to music and stay with the rhythm. Then try it on the left side.

2

◄ THE CAMEL

Remember the Pelvic Camel from chapter 5? If not, go back and learn the Pelvic Camel, as it is the foundation for the full Camel.

Benefit: The Camel is one of the most important moves in bellydance, and healthwise, it is perhaps the most beneficial. The Camel consists of undulating the entire body in a snakelike manner, similar to the Snake Arms we learned earlier. The snakelike movement of the body will stretch, tone, and strengthen the entire torso, front and back. People with sciatic nerve (lower back) problems rave about how this exercise helped rid them of their symptoms. It increases flexibility of the spine and strengthens the muscles responsible for good posture and back support, while firming the upper and lower abdominals. It is one of the hardest moves for a beginner to master, but it is one of the best and definitely worth the time and effort.

1

Starting from standing position with feet together and good posture,

1. Push the rib cage forward.

2. Lift the rib cage up.

3. Push the rib cage back into the body, so that the shoulder blades begin to separate to accommodate the rib cage.

4. Pull the lower abdominals in to make the hips go back. Your pelvis should tuck underneath you. (The pelvic tuck creates a rounding out of the lower back, which is essential for the shape of the Camel.)

5. As soon as your hips go back, begin with step 1 again and push the chest forward.

6. Repeat steps 1–5 continuously so that whenever the chest is pushed out forward, the lower abdominals are pulled in, with pelvis tucked. The pelvis and rib cage should always oppose each other. When one is forward, the other is back, like a snake.

Tip

Once you get the hang of it, focus on making the movement smooth. A key point to remember is to make sure you pull in your lower abdominals for that pelvic tuck. It makes a big difference in the overall look of the movement. Also, practice in front of a mirror to constantly check your form. Some students will stand with their back against a wall and try the exercise, using the wall to check their position. If the shoulder blades are touching the wall, the hips should not be, and if the lower back is touching the wall, the chest should be forward.

3   4   5 6

◄ REVERSE CAMEL

Same as the Camel, but upside down. In a Reverse Camel, the movement starts with a Pelvic Camel and ends at the chest.

1. Starting with the knees bent, push the hips forward and straighten the legs.

2. Then push the chest forward and lift the chest up.

3. As soon as you lift the chest up, pull in the lower abdominals to make the hips move back, bending the knees at the same time.

4. Repeat steps 1–4 so that you develop a smooth undulation.

1   2   3

Chapter 7 | *Traveling Steps*

Exploring Traveling Steps

Several of bellydancing's traveling steps involve adding footwork to some of the basic isolation moves, such as in the Hip Circle Walk or Hip Drop Walk. Others are steps unto themselves, such as the Grapevine. In either case, one of the most important things about traveling steps is to have good form in your footwork. Perform each step in the mirror, and check your form against the step-by-step photos. * One common footwork error is taking too wide a step (remember, feet are always very close together in this dance). A general rule of thumb is to take as small steps as possible with the feet, yet exaggerate the hip movement. Please note that in the photos for this chapter, I am taking larger steps than I normally would, to better illustrate each phase of the movement. * Another mistake is improper foot position, such as having an inward rotation of the foot (pigeon-toes). Always check your form in the mirror!

1   2

HIP SLIDE WALK ▲

Benefit: Works the outer thighs and hips.
If you are in demi-pointe, it will also work
the calves.

Simply walk forward (or backward), and
each time you step with the right foot, slide
the hips out to the right. Each time you step
left, slide the hips to the left. Remember that
this movement is horizontal only, so the hips
should not go up or down at all, just slide
right and left along an imaginary line. This
step can be performed in demi-pointe or
with feet flat on the floor.

1. Step with the right foot while sliding
    the right hip horizontally out to the right.

2. Step with the left foot while sliding the
    left hip horizontally out to the left.

ARABESQUE WALK ▼

Benefit: Works the quadriceps and calves.

Since most bellydance music is in 4/4 timing, we can address the Arabesque Walk in terms of timing. Simply step (preferably in demi-pointe) your right foot on the count of 1; your left foot on the count of 2; then on the count of 3, step right but lift the left foot into passé, lift the left hip slightly, and hold this position for the fourth count. So the count is 1, 2, 3, and hold on 4. You are then ready to step with the left foot on the count of 1. So it's right, left, right, hold; then left, right, left, hold, and so on.

1. Step forward on the right foot.

2. Step forward on the left foot.

3. Step forward on the right foot while lifting the left foot into passe and lifting the left hip.

4. Hold position from step 3 for the fourth count. You are ready to begin the same sequence on the left by stepping on the left foot on the next count of one.

Variation

Instead of lifting the foot into passé and lifting the hip on the 3rd count, you can lift the entire leg and hip straight out in back with the toe pointed.

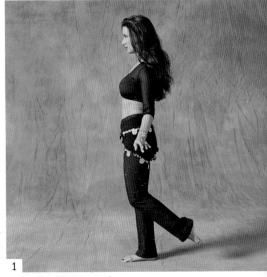

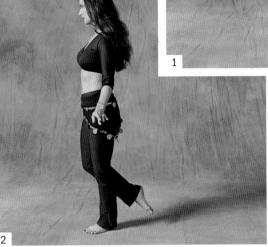

RIGHT-LEFT-RIGHT, LEFT-RIGHT-LEFT

We will find this sequence in several traveling steps, so it is essential to master the footwork first, then learn the variations. In the Arabesque Walk above, we had a right-left-right, left-right-left sequence where we walked forward, alternating feet. In this next version of a right-left-right, left-right-left sequence, we walk front with the right, then weight change back on the left, then forward on the right again. We pause on the fourth count just as we did in the Arabesque Walk. So, the feet are moving right-left-right, left-right-left, and the weight change of the body is front-back-front, front-back-front.

ADVANCED HIP SLIDE WALK

Benefit: The traveling footwork works the legs and feet, while the hip work improves flexibility and tones the hips.

The Advanced Hip Slide Walk uses the R-L-R, L-R-L footwork, with the front-back-front weight change. Now, each time your weight changes to the right, slide your hip to the right (as we did in the Hip Slide). Then, each time you weight change to the back, return the hip to the center. So, the hips are leaning into the direction of the weight change, as follows: right-center-right, left-center-left. You can travel either forward or backward with this step. This step can be done with feet flat on the floor or in demi-pointe.

1. Step forward onto the right foot so that all your weight is on the right.

2. Step backward onto the left foot so that all your weight is on the left.

3. Step forward on the right again.

4. Bring left foot from the back to the front and step forward onto the left foot.

5. Step backward onto the right foot.

6. Step forward onto the left foot.

7. Repeat the above sequence.

Now that you've practiced the footwork, let's add the different variations of hip movements that get layered over the footwork.

1. Step forward onto the right foot while sliding the right hip directly out to the right.

2. Step backward onto the left foot while sliding the right hip back to centered position.

3. Step forward onto the right foot while sliding the right hip directly out to the right.

4. Repeat on the left side.

1. Step onto the right foot while twisting the right hip forward. Do not move hip up or down, as this is strictly a horizontal movement.

2. Step onto the left foot while twisting the right hip to the back.

3. Step onto the right foot while twisting the right hip forward.

4. On the fourth count, bring the left leg from the back in passé toward the front so that you are ready to step on the left on the next count of 1.

1

2

TWIST WALK ▲

Benefit: The traveling footwork works the legs and feet, while the hip work tones the hips and waistline. You will feel it in your waist.

Same as the Advanced Hip Slide Walk, but instead of sliding the hips directly out to the right and left, the hips twist while the feet perform the basic R-L-R, L-R-L footwork. When you step right, twist the right hip forward. When you step left (and weight change to the back) the right hip twists to the back, and so on. So, the hips will twist right/front, right/back, right/front, then left/front, left/back, left/front. This movement is best performed in demi-pointe.

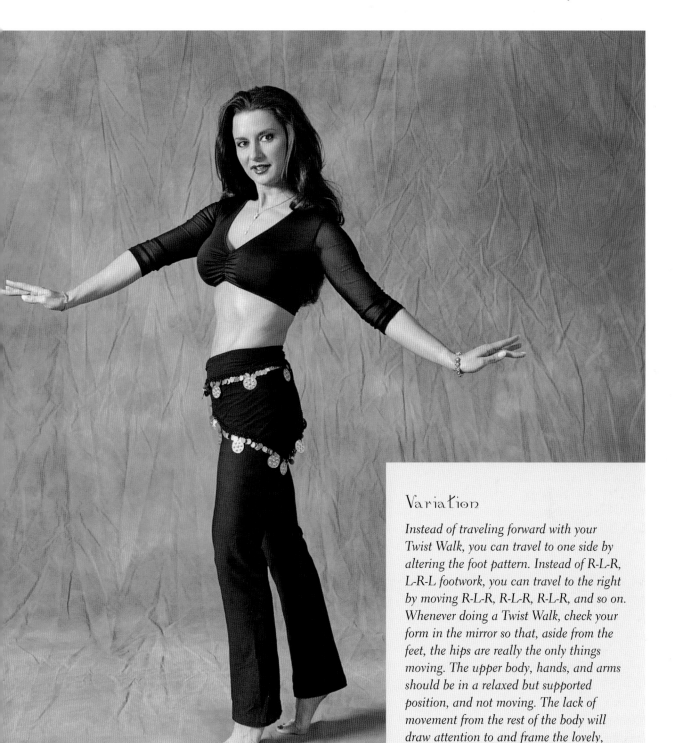

3

Variation

Instead of traveling forward with your Twist Walk, you can travel to one side by altering the foot pattern. Instead of R-L-R, L-R-L footwork, you can travel to the right by moving R-L-R, R-L-R, R-L-R, and so on. Whenever doing a Twist Walk, check your form in the mirror so that, aside from the feet, the hips are really the only things moving. The upper body, hands, and arms should be in a relaxed but supported position, and not moving. The lack of movement from the rest of the body will draw attention to and frame the lovely, twisting hip movement.

1. Step forward on the right while pushing the chest out.

2. Step back onto the left while returning the chest to neutral position.

3. Step forward on the right while pushing the chest out.

4. Bring left leg from back to front to prepare to step on the left on the next count of 1. As you bring the left leg over, keep the knee lifted and the toe pointed, like a horse would.

5. Repeat on left and continue alternating.

HORSE WALK ▲

Benefit: The traveling footwork works the legs and feet, while the upper torso work improves flexibility and tones upper abdominals and rhomboids.

There are several steps from Egyptian dance referred to as Horse steps. In a region of Upper Egypt known as the Fellahi region, where there are a lot of farms and horses, they teach the horses to "dance" using steps similar to those in dressage. Thus, some of the regional folkloric dance steps involve imitating the dancing horses. Hence, the Horse Walk. Using the same R-L-R, L-R-L footwork to travel forward, each time you weight change to the front leg, push your rib cage forward. Each time you weight change to the back leg, the rib cage returns to normal position. So, while the feet are moving R-L-R, L-R-L, the chest is moving front-back-front, front-back-front. Keep an image in your mind of a horse stepping in dressage. As you move your back leg to the front, think of lifting the knee and pointing the toe, the way a horse would move. To have good form lifting the knees, keep support in your lower abdominals. So, during a count of four, the steps would be:

3

Variations

Instead of moving the rib cage forward and back with each weight change, you can lift the chest up and down. Or, you can push the stomach out and in, moving in and out of a Pelvic Tuck.

Also, consider a different arm position, such as arms overhead.

HORSE WALK BACKWARD

The same principal applies for traveling backward with the horse step, except that it is typical to emphasize the lifting of the knee and pointing of the toe at the end of each front-back-front sequence. So, in a count of four, the steps would be:

2

1. Step back onto the right foot while dropping the chest.

2. Step forward onto the left foot while lifting the chest.

3. Step back onto the right while dropping the chest, and lift the left knee and point toe.

3

4. Hold position of step 3 for the fourth count. Keep lower abdominals tucked for support.

5. Repeat on left.

4

1

◄ PELVIC CAMEL WALK (Backward)

Benefit: This traveling step is great for strengthening the lower abdominals and lower back.

Here we layer a Pelvic Camel over the back-front-back footwork. This move has a soft undulation of the pelvis while traveling backward.

1. Step backward onto the right foot while pulling in on the lower abdominals, thus rounding out the lower spine.

2. Step forward onto the left foot while pushing the hips forward by squeezing the buttocks.

3. Step backward onto the right foot while pulling in on the lower abdominals, rounding out the lower spine.

4. On the fourth count, bring the left leg from front to back so that you are ready to step back onto the left on the next count of one.

2

3

4

1 2

THE GRAPEVINE ▲

Benefit: Involves the outer and inner thighs.

This step originates in Greek dancing, but it has spread to many different dance styles. It is also a main staple in aerobic dance choreography, because it is low impact and really gets the heart rate going. This step involves traveling right and left with a footwork pattern.

1. Cross the right foot over and in front of the left.

2. Step to the left with the left foot so the feet are no longer crossed.

3. Cross the right foot behind the left.

4

3

Variation

In step 4, when you touch the toe to the floor, add a hip accent. So the steps would be:

1. Cross left over right.

2. Step right.

3. Cross left behind right.

4. Touch right and push right hip up.

5. Start from step 1 in the other direction by crossing the right foot in front of the left.

4. Uncross the left foot by moving it to the left and touching the toe to the floor, without actually stepping on it.

5. You are ready to repeat the sequence in the other direction by crossing the left foot over the right.

3

1, 2

RIGHT FOOT FORWARD, RIGHT FOOT BACK

As the name suggests, this traveling step involves a step forward and a step backward with the right foot. Obviously, it can also be performed with the left foot. It is common in Middle Eastern dance choreography to perform this step facing forward, then pivoting and facing the right wall, then the back, and so on, so that you travel in the shape of a box.

1. Hands in basic position, stand with feet together but weight on the left, ready to move the right foot.

2. Step in front with the right foot, putting all your weight on the right.

3. Step on the left, putting all your weight on the left, while lifting the right foot into passe.

4. Step back onto the right, putting all your weight on the right.

5. Repeat.

5

4

Variations

• Use this step to travel sideways: When the right foot comes forward, place it forward to the right, then catch up with the left when you step back on the left, so you are performing the step and scooting sideways at the same time.

• Add a level change by bending the supporting (left) leg into plié as the right foot steps forward.

• Layer a shimmy over this step by moving your knees loosely and rhythmically while you go through the steps.

• Add a Hip Lift as you step both forward and back on the right foot.

• Add an arm movement to the step by crossing your hands in front of you as the right foot steps forward, then uncrossing the hands back to basic position as you step back on the right.

1   2

HIP DROP WALK ▲

Benefit: The traveling footwork works the legs and feet, while the hip work improves flexibility and coordination and tones and stretches the hips.

Do just what the name suggests: walk with a Hip Drop.

Variation: Hip Lift Walk

Same as the Hip Drop Walk, but instead of dropping the hip in step 3, you lift the hip.

1. Step forward on the right foot.

2. Bring the left foot forward and point the toes. Keep the left knee slightly bent so that the hip is not lifted by pointing the toes.

3. Lift the left hip by straightening the left knee.

4. Step down onto the left.

1. Step forward onto the right foot.

2. Bring the left foot forward and touch the toe to the floor, without putting your weight onto that foot.

3. Since the left foot is pointed, the left hip should be lifted. Drop the left hip by bending the knee (keep the toes pointed).

4. Step down onto the left foot.

5. Bring right foot to the front and point right foot, without putting your weight on the right.

6. Drop right hip.

7. Step down onto the right foot. Keep repeating the above sequence: step right, point left, drop left hip, step left, or, step, point, drop, step, point, drop, and so on.

8. Repeat on the other side.

3

4

5

6

HIP CIRCLE WALK

This is a lateral traveling step that layers a Hip Circle over a Vamp Step. It takes a bit of practice and coordination, but the step has a nice look and is great exercise for the lower abdominals and lower back. Let's break down the steps for the footwork, or Vamp Step, then layer the Hip Circle over it.

Benefit: The sideways-traveling footwork works the outer and inner thighs, while the hip work really stretches and tones the hips and lower back.

1

2   3

◀ Vamp Step

1. Step sideways to the right with the right foot, putting all your weight on the right.

2. Catch the left foot up to the right so they are close next to each other again, with weight evenly distributed on both feet.

3. Step to the right again with the right foot.

4. Catch the left foot up to the right, but don't put any weight on the left foot—just point the toes of the left foot as you bring the left foot next to the right in passe.

5. Repeat steps 1–4 in the other direction by stepping sideways to the left with the left foot, and so on.

    So, it's step out, step together, step out, and point the toes; repeat other direction.

4

1   2
3

Now, let's layer the Hip Circle movement over the Vamp Step:

Hip Circle Walk ▶

1. Step sideways to the right and make a half circle forward (from left to right) with the hips.

2. Catch the left foot up to the right while completing the hip circle by making a half-circle in the back.

3. Step out with the right and make a half circle with hips in front.

4. When the left foot catches up and points, your hips should be centered, ready to move in the opposite direction.

    So, while the feet are moving step-together-step-point, the hips are moving half circle front, half circle back, half circle front, center.

Tips

- Even though we break the movement down into half circles, keep the traveling movement smooth and rhythmic so that the hips are moving in an even circle.
- Focus on distributing the emphasis of the hips evenly from front to back. A common mistake beginners make is to focus more on the front half of the circle than on the back half, so the movement looks lopsided.
- This step looks great when performed in demi-pointe, with the feet taking very small steps.

LATERAL HIP DROP WALK ▼

Benefit: The sideways-traveling footwork works the outer and inner thighs, while the lateral hip work tones and defines the waist.

Another side-to-side traveling step, the Lateral Hip Drop Walk has a somewhat similar foot pattern to the Hip Circle Walk. In this example we will travel to the right, but obviously, you can also travel to the left by reversing the foot pattern.

 1

 2

3 4

1. Start by standing with the left foot flat on the floor and the right toes pointed and right hip lifted, as if you are about to do a stationary Hip Drop. Instead of having the right foot directly out in front, position it slightly to the right.

2. Step onto the right foot, toes still pointed, and bend the knee to drop the hip.

3. Straighten the right knee to lift the hip again (right toes are still pointed). As the right hip is lifting, slide the left foot over to catch up with the right.

4. Repeat the above sequence, so that as the right hip is moving up and down and up down, the feet are stepping right and catching up left.

Variation

Add an extra Hip Drop with each step. Here's how:

1. Starting on the right, drop the right hip as you step on the right.

2. Catch up the left foot as you lift the right hip again.

3. Without moving the feet at all, drop and lift the right hip one more time.

4. Repeat the above three steps.

Keep repeating the combination as you travel to the right. You can repeat these same steps in the other direction as well.

1

2

4

◀ PHARAONIC WALK

Benefit: Use this traveling step to work the buttocks, quadriceps, and hamstrings.

Although this movement is one of the most used and most beautiful traveling steps in Middle Eastern dance, it happens to be the one a lot of Hollywood types use in their rendition of how they think people danced during the time of the Pharaohs. It involves pushing the back hip up with the back leg in a modified Vamp Step. To travel to the right, the left foot will always have toes pointed, as if you were wearing one high-heeled shoe. (This movement is sometimes called the Lame Duck.)

3

1. Point the toes of your left foot, but keep a slight bend in the left knee so that the hips are level with each other.

2. Straighten the left leg with the toes still pointed, so the left hip lifts.

3. At the same time that the left hip is lifting, step flat onto the right.

4. Catch the left foot up to the right and drop the left hip, keeping the left toe pointed.

5. Keep repeating the above point/lift (L) and step (R); catch up/drop (L).

Variations

There are several variations of hand and arm positions for this step:
Another variation is to layer a shimmy over the step.

1. Diagonal arms

2. Palms up in front

3. Palms up high in front

4. Palms down, hands together

1

2

◀ THE 3/4 SHIMMY

Benefit: The traveling footwork works the legs and feet, while the hip work improves flexibility and coordination and tones and stretches the hips.

Sometimes called a Shimmy Walk, this step is basically layering a shimmy over a regular walking pattern. I prefer to perform this walk in demi-pointe, but it can also be done flat-footed.

1. Step onto the right foot, bending the right knee slightly so the right hip drops slightly.

2. Lift and drop the right hip slightly one more time for good measure.

3. Step onto the left foot, bending the left knee slightly so the left hip drops slightly.

4. Lift and drop the left hip again before repeating on the right.

5. Keep repeating the step/drop and lift/drop sequence for each step that you take.

Tips

If someone was watching you perform this movement from the knees up, without seeing your feet, your hips would just be uniformly bouncing up and down in a small, steady, repetitive movement. The feet just happen to be stepping with every other bounce. So, regardless of what your feet are doing, whether they are stepping or in between steps, the hips are fluid and even. It should really be all about the hips, so check your look in the mirror.

3

4

5

6

1. Step forward onto the left foot as you lean your chest forward, then up.

2. Slide the right foot forward in front of the right as you lean your chest back, then pull in on your lower abdominals. (Your weight is still on the left at this point, but your right foot is forward.)

3. When your chest comes forward again, step with your weight on the right.

4. Repeat each step above, so that each time your chest comes forward, you are alternating which foot you step on.

1 2

CAMEL WALK (Forward) ▲

Benefit: This step has all the wonderful abdominal and back-building benefits of the Camel, with added benefit to the legs and feet, which facilitate the traveling.

Once you have mastered the Camel, it's time to think about traveling with the Camel. Let's break the Camel down into two steps to make learning the traveling part easier.

Think of the first step of the Camel as when you lean your chest forward, then up. Think of step 2 of the Camel as when you lean your chest to the back and pull in on your lower abdominals. Once you can imagine the two steps, it's time to add the feet:

3

◀ CAMEL WALK (Sideways)

Walking laterally with a Camel is quite similar to walking forward with a Camel. The main (and perhaps only) difference is that you do not alternate feet with every forward thrust of the chest. Here is the breakdown:

1

2

1. Step forward and slightly to the left with the left foot, as you push the chest out, then up.

2. Step with the right so the right foot crosses behind the left as you complete the second half of the Camel. Your weight is on the right foot.

3. Step to the left with the left foot (so the feet are no longer crossed) as you perform the first half of the Camel.

4. Repeat the above steps so that you are changing weight front and back, left and right, with each half of the Camel. It should feel as though you are rocking slightly back and forth with each half of the Camel, and the crossing and uncrossing of the feet facilitate the lateral travel.

3

Variations

You can vary the arm/hand positions several ways:

1. Both hands/arms overhead

2. L-shaped arms

3. Both arms down and to the back

4. Hands in hair

Chapter 8 | *Turns, Turns, Turns*

Spins and Turns

Turns are an essential part of just about every form of dance. Bellydance, with all its folkloric roots, is a melting pot for turns that came from whirling dervish dance, Zar (trance) dance, temple dances, and so on, and influences from other countries and dance styles. ✳ There are two key aspects of successful turning: spotting and concentration. Spotting involves looking at a spot or object before beginning a turn, looking at it for as long as you can while you begin the turn, then whipping your head around to lock your gaze onto the exact same spot upon completion of the turn. This will ensure that your turn goes in the direction that you choose, it will give your turn a distinct beginning and end, and it will help prevent dizziness. Concentration is important also, which is probably why turning works so well for trance dances. To successfully spot, maintain rhythm, and keep good form of the body, the mind literally has to slow down and focus on all these aspects. Good-quality, repetitive turning is like being in a meditative state. Many dancers find it helpful to count along with the beat of the music—1, 2, 3, 4, 1, 2, 3, 4—finding their spot on each count of 1.

1

2

THE PADDLE TURN ▼

The Paddle Turn is the most basic turn you can do. It is a very good choice if you are dancing on a surface that is not the most level or smooth, or if you are in a lighting situation where spotting may be difficult. Because the Paddle Turn involves keeping one leg anchored to the ground while the other leg "paddles" around it, the anchoring of the leg can be a substitute for visual spotting.

1. Stand with right foot flat, weight on the right, left foot pointed to the side.

2. Slide the left foot to the front.

3. Push away with the left foot, causing the right foot to pivot a quarter turn.

4. Repeat steps 2 and 3, until you have completed three quarter turns and are facing front again, which is a complete turn. Your weight will always be on the right leg, with the left leg just pushing off.

Tip

Count to the music, one beat for each step/pivot.

3   continued

continued

Variations

Because the Paddle Turn has the advantage of that anchored leg, it is easy to add variations to this turn, such as:

- *Tilting your head to one side as you turn.*

- *Bending the knees slightly for a low Paddle Turn. (You can alternate low and high.)*

BASIC TURN IN PLACE

1. Find a spot directly in front of you to focus on.

2. Rotate the right leg so that the inner thigh is turned out to the front and the right foot faces the right back corner.

3. Step on the right foot.

4. Rotate the left foot to catch up with the right.

5. Step on the left foot.

6. Continue rotating one foot and catching up with the other until you have completed a full circle, facing front again. You should be able to complete a full turn in four steps: right, left, right, left.

7. Find your spot each time you face front.

1

4

PIVOT TURN IN PLACE ▶

1. Stand in demi-pointe facing front, and find your spot.

2. To turn to the right, pivot on the ball of the right foot so that you are facing the back wall. The left foot will automatically follow.

3. Pivot again in the same direction until you face front and find your spot.

6

CHAÎNÉS [SHEH-NAY] ▶

Chaînés means "chain." This turn involves a series of half turns in succession, which would resemble links in a chain. It absolutely requires spotting, and is a great turn for traveling in a straight line.

1, 2

To Chaînés to the left:

1. Turn your head to the left and find a spot to focus on.

2. Point the left foot to get ready to step.

3. Make a half turn to the left by pivoting on the left foot, so you are facing the back wall. Keep your eyes on your spot on the left wall.

4. Make one more half turn in the same direction by pivoting on the same foot, keeping your eyes on the spot. You have completed one turn.

4

3

Variations

To travel in a straight line, keep repeating steps 1–4 (look, step, half turn, half turn), maintaining focus on your spot the entire time.

To travel in a circle, change your spot to a different wall after each turn, such as right, back, left, and front. This involves a lot of concentration, because you have to find your spot quickly.

BARREL TURN ▼

The Barrel Turn is difficult, but so worth it. The footwork on the Barrel Turn is essentially the same as the Basic Turn in Place, but the upper body position changes. If I am turning clockwise, I prefer to begin my footwork with the left foot.

3

4

1, 2

1. Step forward onto left foot, so that it is almost crossing over the right.

2. Lean your upper body forward as you perform step 1, dipping your left arm toward the floor.

3. Rotate the right leg so that the inner thigh is turned out to the front and the right foot faces the right back corner.

4. Rotate the left foot to catch up with the right. You should now be facing the back wall. Because your upper body is still tilted, by the time you reach step 4, your chest should be facing up to the ceiling.

5. Step with the right foot facing the left wall.

6. You are ready to begin the sequence again with step 1 by stepping front with the left and dipping the left arm down.

6

1   2

◀ CROSSOVER TURN

This is one of my favorite turns because it is relatively easy to do and is visually interesting.

To turn counterclockwise:

1. Lift the right foot into passé.

2. Cross the right foot over and in front of the left, and place it next to the left.

3. Uncross your legs by pivoting to the back.

4. Pivot again to make one half turn, returning to the front.

Variations

You can also perform this turn backward. Instead of crossing the right foot in front of the left, cross it from behind. The rest of the steps are the same.

To give this turn a more ethnic or folkloric look, during step 1 where you lift the right foot into passé, also lift the right hip, and tilt the upper body toward the lifted hip. The rest of the turn is the same, but the lifting of the hip and the tilt of the upper body really change the look of the turn.

Chapter 9 | *Balancing and Floor Movements*

Balancing

For thousands of years, dancers have been performing bellydance moves while balancing such things as candelabras with lighted candles, silver trays topped with votive candles, swords, vases, jugs, and probably the kitchen sink. Balancing is the ultimate demonstration of a dancer's ability to perform isolation exercises. If she is truly isolating, the movement of each of her body parts will not affect any other body part. So, she should be able to fully dance while keeping her head still and level. ✳ Floor movements are almost always incorporated into any dance that involves balancing, to show a dancer's skill.

Floor Movements

Some bellydance movements are performed on the floor, either to add height changes for choreographic dynamics, or to show a dancer's strength. Some movements, such as doing Belly Rolls on the floor, originated in childbirth preparation exercises. Regardless of where they come from, they certainly can add spice to a dance routine.

Benefit: Floor movements depend on the strength of the trunk of the body (core strength) to execute movement. The arms and legs are used mainly for support and steering. Building core strength and developing good floor technique involve good visualization, concentration, and control.

Floor movements are not easy, and not recommended at all for people with knee problems. Floor movements require a lot of strength, so dancers must remember to keep a relaxed face regardless of how much effort they are exerting.

CAMEL ON THE FLOOR ▲

This movement involves balancing yourself on one leg and arm, and undulating the body in the most graceful way possible. Remember to keep nice hand position and point the toes.

ODALISQUE ▾

Odalisque is simply a series of poses on
the floor. The real exercise is getting
into and out of the pose, which really
depends on core strength.

1. From a kneeling position, lean your upper body slowly back
   until your head and shoulders are resting on the floor. You will
   need control in your abdominals and support in your quadriceps to do this. You do not have to arch your back; you can
   just gently lower yourself into this position. Your arms should
   be above your head, as pictured.

2. Bring your arms out to your sides.

3. Return your arms to their position above your head.

4. Slowly lift your upper body, quadriceps first, back to a kneeling or sitting position.

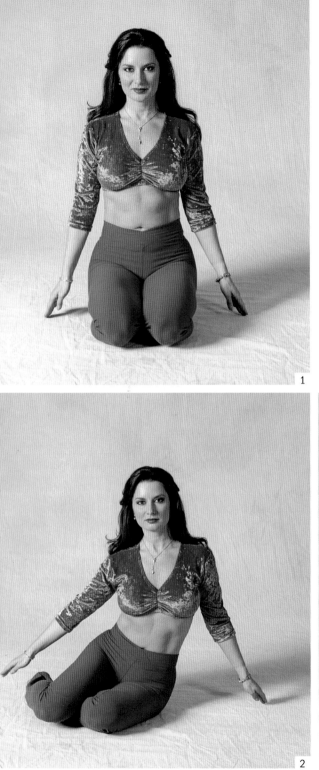

SEATED TURN

This is really neat way to get around while on the floor, especially if you happen to be balancing something on your head. Please do not even attempt this movement if you have any kind of knee problems, as this step relies totally on the knees.

1. Sit on the floor so that you are sitting on your heels.

2. Nudge your bottom to the left and sit on it, so that you are sitting with your bottom on the floor and feet to the right of your bottom.

2   3

3. Extend legs by straightening the knees. Your body will automatically rotate beneath you, so that you are now facing 90 degrees to the right of where you were facing in step 1.

4. Bend your knees so that you bring your feet to the left of your bottom.

5. Lift yourself to a kneeling position with your feet directly beneath you. You will now automatically be facing 90 degrees of where you were in step 3.

6. Repeat steps 1–5 until you have made a full circle.

4

5

2

◀ FULL TURN ON THE FLOOR

Here is a fun way to roll around on the floor and get back up while still looking graceful. This movement utilizes and develops core strength in the trunk of the body, as you have to lean the torso in various directions to facilitate the movement without the help of your arms or legs.

1

3 4

1. From a standing position, bend into a kneeling position.

2. Put your right arm on the floor next to you, and extend your left arm and leg into the pose pictured.

3. Lean the front of your body forward, extending both arms and legs out straight, so that you are lying on your tummy.

5

4. Keeping your arms and legs extended, roll over onto your back.

5. Bend your knees so that your feet are behind you.

6. Lift your body back into a sitting or kneeling position.

6

154 ✳ *Belly*dancing for Fitness

◂ UNDULATING, KNEELING BACK BEND

Yes, this really is as difficult as it looks. So why do it? Because I have never found an exercise that works the quadriceps and abdominals as well as this one. If you have no known knee problems, just attempting this movement two or three times will make you aware of muscles you didn't know you had. This movement is also fascinating to watch.

5

1. Begin in a kneeling position with feet shoulder-width apart.

2. Keeping *lots* of support in your quadriceps and abdominals, arch your back and gradually bring the top of your head toward the floor behind you.

3. Inches before your head reaches the floor, change directions by aiming your head forward and pulling your abdominals in hard (similar to the Camel).

4. Continue directing your head and chest forward, while your hips stay behind you.

5. Finish in kneeling position.

Chapter 10 | *Dancing with a Veil*

A Gorgeous Upper-Body Workout

Dancing with a veil serves two purposes for the professional dancer: it is a reflection of Arabic culture, reminiscent of shawls and Islamic head and face coverings, and it is a big block of color that makes a dancer's entrance large and attention-getting. ✳ Proper veil technique involves keeping support in the arms at all times, and never letting the veil droop or fall to the floor (unintentionally, that is). The best approach to working with a veil is to really think about carving shapes in the air with your arms, so the veil will echo these shapes. Also, it is important to remember to move briskly to keep air underneath the veil so that it does not sag during movement.

Benefit: Working with a veil is an excellent upper-body workout. It works the entire upper body, and works the arms and shoulders in their full range of motion. It is great for developing posture, and for working away upper-body tension.

Here are some photographs illustrating some common veil techniques:

Arabesque Walk
while lifting veil

The Sail: holding the veil with one arm pointing up and the other in front of the body, while turning

Circling the veil around the head

Barrel Turn with veil

Turning while wearing the veil "Butterfly" style

Chapter 11 | *The Next Step:*
Layered Movements, Combinations, and Routines

Layering Movements

Now that you have mastered the basic movements and traveling steps, you are ready to start layering or combining two or more movements simultaneously. This requires some compartmentalization of the brain: you may have to dedicate one section of your brain to one movement, another section of your brain to another movement, and yet another section of your brain to make sure your face doesn't show how confused your brain is.

Layering Movements

Here are a few examples of advanced layering of movements that you can try:

Camel over an Egyptian Shimmy: Start by getting good rhythm going with an Egyptian Shimmy. Devote one section of your brain to maintaining the shimmy, while another section of your brain leads you into a Camel. Practice making nice, smooth Camels while keeping a constant, steady shimmy rhythm. You can also do this with a Reverse Camel.

Hip Circle or Horizontal Figure Eight over an Egyptian Shimmy: Just as with the Camel/Shimmy, practice in the mirror, making sure you are executing the movements correctly and gracefully while keeping your shimmy steady.

Snake Arms over a Shimmy: Shimmy away while focusing on making continuous Snake Arm undulations in the frontal plane. If you really want to challenge yourself, try to Camel, Shimmy, and do Snake Arms at the same time. You can also do Snake Arms while traveling laterally with a Choo Choo.

Shimmy over a Pharaonic Walk: Start traveling with the Pharaonic Walk from chapter 7. Once you have established a rhythm, think about making small, rubbery, back-and-forth shaking movements with your knees while you are traveling, so that there is a constant shimmy going on beneath your movement.

Right Foot Forward, Right Foot Back, Hands Cross and Uncross, with Shimmy: As you step forward with the right foot, bring your hands to the front and cross them. As you bring the right foot back, uncross your hands and bring them back to the basic position. As you step with your feet, keep your knees moving in a steady rhythm so that your hips are shimmying constantly. Repeat this four times, facing a different direction each time: front, left, back, and right.

Hip Circle over a Choo Choo: Start with a Choo Choo by shimmying while you are in demi-pointe. Establish the rhythm of your shimmy. Then, add the hip circle by gently leaning your hips to the right, front, left, and back, while still shimmying. This movement works best when traveling laterally.

Head Slide over a Choo Choo: Start with your Choo Choo. Your knees will be shimmying back and forth at least four times for each head slide. As you Choo Choo laterally, slide your head to the right and left.

Hip Circle Walk while Turning: Start with your Hip Circle Walk from chapter 7. Instead of just taking a step sideways with each half circle of the hips, you take a step and pivot the foot, so that with each half circle of the hips, you face a different direction. You should be able to make a 360-degree turn in four steps: right, left, right, left, while completing two hip circles.

Shoulder Shimmy over a Grapevine: Start with the Grapevine from chapter 7 and add a steady Shoulder Shimmy (gentle shaking of the shoulders). Whenever using a Shoulder Shimmy, make sure you have nice posture, or it will look . . . strange, to say the least. No drooping!

Hands Crossed on Ascent, Open on Descent over Egyptian Shimmy: Self-explanatory. Lovely hand movements are layered over a steady shimmy. Keep a relaxed face.

Snake Arms with Rib Slides: As you slide your rib cage to the right, undulate your right arm so that it has the appearance that the lifting of your elbow is pulling your rib cage to the side. Repeat on the left. As you alternate right and left, your upper body (rib cage and arms) will be swaying side to side. Keep the rest of your body still.

Those are just a few suggestions, since there is an endless list of possible moves that can be combined. They all take practice, as does everything that has to do with bellydance. Figure out which ones work best for you!

Combinations

Combinations are a series of consecutive movements. It is entirely necessary to count while working on a combination. Ask any musician, music is all about counting the beats, and so is dance (especially choreographed dance). If you are not familiar with counting, spend a few moments listening to your favorite song, or to the CD included with this book, and just count along with the beats. Try to find the "1," which means try to find the point at which a new measure starts. This happens usually every four or eight beats (if the music has 4/4 timing), for example, 1, 2, 3, 4, 1, 2, 3, 4, and so on.

When you are familiar with counting, practice some of your favorite moves while counting to the beat of the music. For example, make sure each of the four steps of a Grapevine lands on a beat and can be counted: 1, 2, 3, 4. Now you can put movements together to the music while counting the beats.

The possibilities are endless. Experiment with moves that seem to transition well from one to another. Also, think about adding variety by mixing steps that travel laterally, forward, backward, diagonally, in a circle, and in place.

---

1. | Grapevine | Turn Right | Choo Choo | Camel | Hip Circle |
   | 1, 2, 3, 4 | 1, 2, 3, 4 | 1, 2, 3, 4 | 1, 2 | 3, 4 |

2. | Pharaonic Walk with Shimmy traveling right | 2 Left Hip Lifts | Repeat other direction. |
   | 1, 2, 3, 4, 5, 6 | 7, 8 | |

3. | Hip Drop Walk Forward | Crossover Turn |
   | 1, 2, 3, 4, 5, 6, | 7, 8 |

4. | Twist Walk Sideways | Reverse Camel | Shimmy | Shoulder Shimmy | Chest Drops | Repeat other direction. |
   | 1, 2, 3, 4, 5, 6 | 7, 8 | 1, 2, 3, 4 | 5, 6 | 7, 8 | |

5. | Pelvic Camel Walk Backward | Reverse Camel | Horse Walk Forward |
   | 1, 2, 3, 4, 5, 6 | 7, 8 | 1, 2, 3, 4, 5, 6, 7, 8 |

6. | 3 Hip Drops (left) | Transition to other hip | 3 Hip Drops (right) | Repeat. |
   | 1, 2, 3, | 4 | 1, 2, 3, transition | |

7. | Shimmy with Snake Arms | Hip Circle | Camel Walk Sideways | 2 Ommis |
   | 1, 2, 3, 4, 5, 6 | 7, 8 | 1, 2, 3, 4, 5, 6 | 7, 8 |

8. | Hip Slide Walk Forward | Twist Walk Sideways to Right | Hip Slide Walk Backward | Twist Walk Sideways to Left |
   | 1, 2, 3, 4, 5, 6, 7, 8 | 1, 2, 3, 4, 5, 6, 7, 8 | 1, 2, 3, 4, 5, 6, 7, 8 | 1, 2, 3, 4, 5, 6, 7, 8 |

9. Lateral Hip Drop Walk Right   Advanced Hip Slide Walk Forward   Lateral Hip Drop Walk Left   Vertical Figure Eights
    1, 2, 3, 4, 5, 6, 7, 8   1, 2, 3, 4   1, 2, 3, 4, 5, 6, 7, 8   1, 2, 3, 4

10. 2 Vertical Figure Eights   2 Camels   2 Rib Circles   4 Ommis
    1, 2, 3, 4   1, 2, 3, 4   1, 2, 3, 4   1, 2, 3, 4

11. 3 Vertical Hip Circles   Reverse Camel   Shoulder Shimmy   2 Pelvic Tucks
    1, 2, 3   4   1, 2   3, 4   Repeat on other side.

12. Hip Circle Walk (right)   4 Hip Drops (left hip)   Hip Circle Walk (left)   4 Hip Drops (right hip)
    1, 2, 3, 4   1, 2, 3, 4   1, 2, 3, 4   1, 2, 3, 4

13. Choo Choo with Snake Arms (right)   Hip Lift Walk (forward)   Horizontal Figure Eight   Horse Walk (backward)   Pivot Turn
    1, 2, 3, 4, 5, 6, 7, 8   1, 2, 3, 4, 5, 6   7, 8   1, 2, 3, 4, 5, 6, 7, 8   1, 2, 3, 4, 5, 6, 7, 8

14. Bounce Shimmy   Twist Shimmy   Bounce Shimmy   Shoulder Shimmy
    1, 2, 3, 4   1, 2, 3, 4   1, 2, 3, 4   1, 2, 3, 4   Repeat.

15. Drop and Kick Right Hip (twice)   Khaleegy Hair Toss (right side)
    1, 2, 3, 4   1, 2, 3, 4   Repeat on left side.

16. Right Foot Forward, Right Foot Back with Shimmy 4x (4 counts each)   Shimmy   Hip Slide Right, then Left   Shimmy   2 Camels
    1, 2, 3, 4, 5, 6, 7, 8, 9, 10, 11, 12, 13, 14, 15, 16   1, 2, 3, 4, 5, 6   7, 8   1, 2, 3, 4   5, 6, 7, 8

Putting Together a Bellydance

Important: Warm up before you work out! See chapter 3 for suggested warm-ups and stretches.

METHOD 1

After trying out the combinations, pick four or five combinations that (a) you really like and (b) work a variety of muscle groups. For example, I might pick #8 because the twisting and hip sliding will work my hips and waist; #1 because the traveling will get my heart rate up; #13 because it works the calves, arms, neck, hips, and torso; #7 because it works the arms, abs, back, and hips; and #5 because it works the lower abs and torso. I would also be inclined to add #12 because the Hip Circles and Hip Drops are essential bellydance moves.

Use the two fitness tracks on the CD that comes with this book. Start with one combination such as #8, and repeat it eight times. Then, add the next

METHOD 2

Another way of constructing a workout is using less combinations but doing more of them. This is great for people who don't like a lot of choreography. Choose four combinations, such as #16, #13, #12, and #9. Start with #16 and repeat eight times. Then take #13 and do it eight times. Then do #16 and #13 together eight times. Next, try #12 eight times. Then do #16, #13, and #12 together eight times. Now try #9 eight times. Last, put all four together and repeat eight times.

I cannot stress enough the importance of counting while dancing combinations or while doing a workout. Aerobics instructors are constantly counting.

Fitness Routine

combination, #1, and do both #8 and #1 together (consecutively) eight times. Add #13, and do #8, #1, and #13 together 8 times. Do the same to add #7, #5, and #12.

If six combinations is too much or too long a workout for you, cut it back to four, and try adding more in a few weeks when you feel stronger from practice. Or, cut the amount of repetitions from eight to five before adding a new combination.

Aside from keeping you in the choreography and keeping you in time with the music, counting during a workout helps you keep track of how many exercises you are doing. Knowing how many repetitions of a given exercise you can do will help you set fitness goals and monitor your progress.
Also, it is important to check your form in the mirror as often as possible. If you are performing the exercises incorrectly, you will not be gaining any of the health benefits from the exercises. Also remember that just because you are counting, it doesn't mean that your movements have to be fast. You can still count but perform the movements at half tempo, taking two counts for each step. Go at your own pace; it's your workout.

Remember that using bellydance moves and combinations for a workout routine is quite different from putting together a dance routine. If you are interested in pursuing bellydance as an art form, consider taking bellydance classes from a reputable instructor and/or buying some instructional or performance videos to understand how to put these moves to music. For working out, our primary focus is to put together movements that will benefit targeted areas of the body. For dancing, one has to learn to interpret the music and understand which movements should naturally follow each other, which is entirely different.

Internet Resources

Here are just a few examples of places on the Internet to find bellydance-related items and information, listed by category.

Costumes

Dahlal Internationale—www.dahlal.com

Audrena's International Bazaar—www.audrena.com

Johara International—www.joharah.com

Isis Imports—www.isisimports.com

Lost Treasures—www.lost-treasures.com

Sheherezade Imports—www.scheherezadeimports.com

Turquoise International—www.turquoiseintl.com

Eclypse Belly Dance Shoppe—www.bellydanceshoppe.com

Diamond Pyramid—www.diamondpyramid.net

Isis—www.isisandthestardancers.com

Neckelmann's—www.neckelmanns.com

Music

Hossam Ramzy—www.hossamramzy.com

Pe-Ko Records—www.pekorecords.com

John Bilezikjian—www.dantzrecords.com

Issam Houshan—www.tablabyissam.com

Souhail Kaspar—www.neareastmusic.com

Amir Sofi—www.amirsofi.com

Solace—www.eventidemusicproductions.com

Dr. Samy Farag—www.sphinxrecords.com

Adam Basma—www.adambasma.com

Ark 21 Records—www.ark21.com

Videos

Little Egypt—www.littleegypt.com

Natural Journeys—www.naturaljourneys.com

IAMED—www.bellydance.org

Dahlal Internationale—www.dahlal.com

Audrena's International Bazaar—www.audrena.com

Pe-Ko Records—www.pekorecords.com

Magazines

Zaghareet—www.zaghareet.com

Jareeda—www.jareeda.com

Habibi—www.habibimagazine.com

The Gilded Serpent—www.gildedserpent.com

Articles and Information

Morocco—www.casbahdance.org

Artemis Mourat—www.serpentine.org

www.discoverbellydance.com

www.bhuz.com

www.bellydanceweb.com

www.hossamramzy.com

www.joyofbellydancing.com

Organizations

Austin Belly Dance Association
(ABDA)—www.abda.org

Atlanta Danse Orientale Society (ADOS)—
www.egyptiannights.org

Arizona Middle Eastern Dance
Association (AMEDA)—www.ameda.net

Middle Eastern Culture and
Dance Association (MECDA)—www.mecda.org

Washington Area Mid-East Dance
Association (WAMEDA)—www.wameda.org

San Diego Area Middle Eastern Dance
Association (SAMEDA)—www.sdsameda.com

Middle Eastern Dance Association of
New Zealand (MEDANZ)—www.medanz.org.nz

Middle Eastern Dance Association of British
Columbia, Canada (MEDA)—www.meda.bc.ca

The North Texas Middle Eastern Dance
Association (NTMEDA)—www.ntmeda.org

Rakkasah—www.rakkasah.com

The Isis Foundation—www.isisandthestardancers.com

Accessories

Some of Rania's clothing used in this book was courtesy of Nourhan Sharif (www.nourhansharif.com).

Some of Rania's hip scarves worn in this book were purchased from Planet Chic (www.planetchic.com) and Natural Journeys (www.naturaljourneys.com).

Visit Rania on the Web for instructional
and performance videos, photos, articles,
and links at www.raniabellydance.com.

Bellydancing Music

© Fair Winds Press

The music on the accompanying CD is a compilation of some of my favorite songs. I've included information on each song to help you find the right mood and tempo with which to practice all of the steps you're learning.

Tabel Ya Issam

Issam Houshan

This original modern composition by Issam is great for composing an advanced bellydance routine. Try to learn all the drum accents.

Issam's Drum Solo

Issam Houshan

This is an original drum solo by Issam. Practice the different types of shimmies and choo choos, and hit the accents with hip drops, chest drops, and locks.

Azziza

Issam Houshan

This song is a remake of a classical Egyptian song. It is great for composing a bellydance routine using lots of turns and traveling steps.

Sallasana

John Bilezekjian

Sallasana, or "wave your handkerchief," is a soulful Turkish Ballad. This is perfect for practicing basic moves and turns, working with a veil, or just for listening.

Old-Style Turkish Medly

John Bilezekjian

This medley is composed of three songs: Mavi Mavi ("Blue Eyes"), Tellegraphin Tellerini ("Birds on a telegraph wire"), and Sivasda ("I love someone from Sivas"). John put the three songs together to make the perfect Turkish-style bellydance routine.

Caravan

The Mogador Band

This song is from Stella Grey's *Bellydancing for Fortune and Fame* CD, a CD made especially for dancers. The slow, steady rhythm of this song is perfect for working on the basic movements, warm-ups, and stretches.

Today My Love

Paul Dinletir

This is workout music! Step into high gear with this music made especially for a bellydance workout, from *Rania's Exotic Bellydance Workout* video.

Fast Hips

Paul Dinletir

Another nonstop bellydance fitness track from "Rania's Exotic Bellydance Workout." Great for traveling steps, shimmies, and lots of choo choos. The steady beat is timed for maintaining your target heart rate.

Empires in the Sand

Time to cool down and stretch to this relaxing track.

All music used with the permission of the artist.

Acknowledgments

This was not a simple book to write, as it treads a thin line between Middle Eastern Dance for fitness, and as a high art form. Many aspects of the dance could not make it into this book, they had to be 'filtered out,' so to speak, to keep to the main concept of fitness and not burden the reader with too much at once. This was incredibly difficult for me, as I am so passionate about this art form, I wanted to include every detail about anything that ever had to do with Bellydancing. Thanks to Donna and Holly at Rockport Publishing/Fair Winds Press for helping me manage and organize the book's content and answering all those questions, and to Rhia for being so helpful about everything.

I am aware that it is impossible to teach a dance form completely with photos and text, and so I hope that readers will use this book as a guide and supplement their learning with quality live instruction and video tapes. Middle Eastern dance has a beautiful and intricate flow that should be witnessed in full motion.

Special thanks to my friends Joyce Ricker and Marina Darowish-Fine for all the 'telephone therapy' sessions, and to Tony Taylor for his unconditional friendship. Thanks also to Haitham (Leo) Mostafa for teaching me to speak Arabic, and for all those song translations and years of loving support. Thanks to Saeed (Steve) from the Seaside Palace where I perform, for standing by me all these years in friendship. Special thanks to Lisa Hoglan, my good friend and assistant, for being there and helping me with just about everything from cat bathing to video production. Thanks also to Dee Dee, Ahmed and Noura Asad, and Amr Kamal of Dallas, Texas.

It is important for me to acknowledge all the dancers and teachers who have been inspirational to me, both as artists and as examples of dedication and professionalism. My gratitude and respect extends to Nancy (Natasha), Lisa (Sheherezat), Serena Wilson, Nicole Michaud, Morocco, Suhaila Salimpour, Angelika Nemeth, Tonya and Atlantis, Sahra Saeeda, Raqia Hassan, Dina, Mona Al Said, Sohair Zaky, Lucy, Nourhan and Yousry Sharif, Fahtiem, Jillina, Eva Cernick, Susanna Delvecchio, Zahra Zuhair, Horatio and Beata Cifuentes, Amir Thaleb, Amar Gamal and Kaeshi, Cassandra, Hadia, and Jehan Kamal.

And of course . . . thanks, mom!

About the Author

Rania Androniki Bossonis is an AFAA certified fitness instructor and professional Middle East dance soloist, choreographer, and master teacher. She has been actively involved in both bellydance and fitness since her junior high school years. She has spent years studying all aspects of Middle Eastern dance, including historical, cultural, and fitness benefits of the dance. She currently teaches Middle Eastern Dance for the Los Angeles Department of Cultural Affairs.

Rania has won numerous awards for the skill and authenticity of her dance in both Egyptian and Turkish/Arabic styles. Rania has over 15 instructional, workout, and performance videos currently available in stores and online, including the smash hit *Bellydance Divas* and her fitness series entitled *Bellydance Fitness for Weight Loss*. She travels throughout the United States and abroad teaching and performing Middle Eastern dance. Her passion for this unique and beautiful art form is evident in both her instruction and performance.